Visualize.
Strategize.
Monetize.

Gina James

Table of Contents

Introduction

My journey started in 2007 when I decided to pursue my first passion—a small business in which I worked as a virtual assistant. I had previously taken a few outsourcing gigs on various sites that offered the service, and they had worked out, so I decided to create my own business.

Roadblock. As soon as I made my first LLC and overpaid for a low-quality website, I realized that the money wasn't coming in the way I had imagined. I wasn't getting any jobs, and I had no idea how to market my business except by posting flyers and leaving cards in restaurants.

So I did what most people do: I gave up.

I re-enrolled in school and pursued my long, boring career in retail once again. Soon after, I became a contractor and had the privilege of touring in Iraq and Afghanistan as part of the effort to support our troops.

Then the oddest thing happened: I was overwhelmed with thoughts of becoming a virtual assistant once more and creating another business. My passion was trying to shine through.

Once again, I went out and paid for a website. This one was a lot better than the first, but it still brought no money to my pocket. To learn where I was going wrong, I began purchasing e-books and other self-help materials to teach me how to monetize my business.

Well, I read books, articles, blogs, and other resources *what* to do, but lacked the basic guidelines on *how* to do it.

After that, I thought I might hire a consultant to get me on track. Numerous times, I hired such individuals, and numerous times, I wasted money. I paid more than $800 a month to get key information but only ended up more confused. Like the material I read, the people I hired told me what to do without telling me how to do it.

That's when I decided I'd had enough of wasting my hard-earned savings and valuable time and ending up nowhere.

I decided to become a certified coach so that I could have the credentials necessary to pass on the guidelines to monetizing businesses. I wanted to ensure that I would be able to guide others in life and business and do so more effectively than the books and individuals who had disappointed me. I wanted to be sure that we would be able to tackle all potential hurdles together. I also became Six Sigma certified. Six Sigma is an organization that uses quality management methods to improve quality output and remove the causes of errors in businesses.

The end result? I started running successful businesses, and I wrote this book to help you do the same. This book not only tells you what to do; it tells you how to do it! My goals are to encourage you to go after your passions and to help you make money.

Here's a quick rundown of my basic principles:

- Making money online is easy when you have guidance.
- Turn a thought into a revenue stream.
- Learn how to utilize affiliate marketing to leverage your residual revenue. Affiliate marketing is also a good business avenue for those who have not created a product.
- Get a basic understanding of how things work, and then tweak your findings to what works for you.
- Never give up. When things go wrong, try again.
- Follow your dreams.

It's both simple and a little bit complicated. This book will guide you through it.

Section One
Visualize

Chapter 1
Accept Who You Are

The Importance of Self-Confidence

When it comes to stepping out, your confidence has a great impact on your success. It is absolutely impossible to step outside of your comfort zone without having a) at least a little confidence, and/or b) a belief that your intentions are for the best and that they are valid.

It's easy to look around at others and feel like we're out of our league. When we do that, though, we end up reverting back to our previous, pre-purpose thoughts, which can defeat our drive and passion.

Do you think that way? Well, STOP! . Those thoughts are damaging and will get in the way of what you really want from life.

Some examples of negative thoughts include:

- "What's the point? It's too hard!"

- "Who am I kidding? I'm not the next Bill Gates."

- "I'll never be able to make money from this. This is such a stupid idea!"

- "What if it doesn't work out? It will just confirm that I'm a loser."

These, or similar thoughts, have crossed everyone's mind at one point or another. Often, these thoughts manifest themselves when you are not confident about where you are in your life.

Lacking self-confidence can have many negative effects on your progress. If you don't believe in yourself, then you most likely won't be willing to follow your passions. By not trying, you're setting yourself back in life and preventing your success. Many people fall into this trap. By not trying, they are never able to discover their true potential, and they deprive the world of their talents.

Take a close look at yourself. Do you have hopes and dreams that you want to make into reality? You are capable of making them happen! Just be willing to step out from behind the walls you have built around yourself and really give your dreams a try. The worst that can happen is that you're not successful . at first. When you don't meet with success, reevaluate your approach and try again. You are worth the effort, and you are capable of doing whatever you set your mind to.

Keyword:

> **Self-confidence:** believing in yourself. The first step to self-confidence is to stop thinking negative and/or defeatist thoughts about yourself.

Accepting Where and Who You Are

When embarking on a new endeavor, it is important to accept yourself as you are, no matter what circumstances you encounter. Accept the fact that you are exactly where you are supposed to be, even though you feel there are improvements that you could make to your life. Every person has had plans that didn't turn out.

Example:

> In your plans, you were supposed to a) stay at your corporate job for twenty years or b) have been a college professor for the last ten years. Accept the fact that a) it's been three years and you still haven't found a job in the field you studied, or b) that you're currently enrolled in college and you don't know what you want to do or be in life. Accept that you don't have a million dollars in the

bank. Even accept the fact that you don't know how you will pay next month's rent.

Everyone struggles with expectations at some point; many wish they had done better. Just remember, no matter what your circumstances are, you can always choose to change your perspective—and thereby change your reality.

Accepting yourself is important because it encourages growth. When you have a clear picture of where you are in life, you have a better understanding of the direction in which you want to go. After years of struggling and wondering, you can see the path you were meant to follow. On the other hand, if you're sitting around with regrets and worries about the future, then you are doing nothing but creating even greater anxieties and stresses. This attitude is totally unnecessary. Give yourself a break!

I like to think of fears as devastating and repetitive experiences. Anxiety is like a virus that comes around every season and knocks out dreams and desires, leaving weakness and self-doubt in its wake—if you let it.

What about you? Do you face anxiety when you are out of your comfort zone? If you do, it's time to break out now!

Keywords:

Perspective: how you view the world and yourself. By changing your perspective, you can change your personal reality.

Reality: the state of affairs and being that is real and actual. Reality is defined both by cultural consensus and by personal perspective. How you perceive your situation and self affects your actual situation and self. In order to change your reality, you need to first change your perspective.

5 Ways to Get Out of Your Comfort Zone:

1. **Try something different every day.** You will never discover new talents and skills unless you take a chance and try something different. A routine can be comforting, but it doesn't foster change. Change can be amazing. You never know unless you try!

2. **Meet someone different every day.** Being around the same people keeps you in your comfort zone. You will miss out on others' insights, logic, and unique personalities by playing it safe and not trying to expand your inner circle. Every single person can bring something unique to your life, which you will miss out on unless you're willing to engage others on a regular basis.

3. **Open up more to others.** Constantly staying in your own comfort zone and creating a shell around yourself makes it difficult for you to learn and grow with others. Your thoughts and opinions count. Make them matter. You are not only limiting yourself by not opening up your ideas to others; you are also hurting yourself and your chances at success.

4. **Offer help to others**. Sometimes it takes more than one person to accomplish a task. You and those you help can grow and learn from helping each other. Don't wait for someone to ask for your help. Put yourself out there and offer your assistance. Remember that some people don't like to ask but appreciate help when they get it!

5. **Know your boundaries and try to step outside of the box.** Venturing outside the boundaries of your comfort zone can be challenging. Jump out of your boundaries and try something new. You never know, it might just be a great talent you have yet to discover!

Comfort zones are just that: comfortable. Great things don't happen when you stay inside your box. Take the time to stretch yourself and your experiences. A lot can be learned about yourself and others by stepping out of your comfort zone. Some of your greatest life experiences might just be waiting right outside your box! Go ahead and find them.

Keyword:

> **Comfort Zone**: also called a "box" or "shell," your comfort zone encompasses the situations and interactions that create within you a safe, easy, in-control feeling. When in your comfort zone, you will have a limited number of thoughts, behaviors, and learning opportunities available, and change will be difficult. One of the first steps to improving your life is to learn how to step out of your comfort zone.

Achieving Change

Now that you have a general idea of how to exit your comfort zone, it's time to evaluate your life and accept what is working and what is not. This process requires you to be brutally honest with yourself. Let's say, for instance, that you are currently enduring a job that you absolutely hate. Say to yourself, "I know this job gives me the chance to support my family, but it's not working!" Now you're ready for change. Acknowledge that you need this change; doing so gives you the power to change it! This is called changing your perspective.

Change is hard. Staying in bad circumstances is worse.

Which would you rather have? A job you dread going to every morning, which barely covers the cost of living . . . or a job you really enjoy, with little to no struggle? Believing that being on a true path to overall happiness and satisfaction is much better than hating your circumstance. Hating your job makes your entire life miserable. People who are not satisfied with their professions often take their negativity home with them, which can affect their relationships and the people around them. Be mindful of this going forward.

What are the things you wish you could change about your personal circumstances? Perhaps you wish you could work from home and spend more time with your family. That looks tricky: the job you have requires massive amounts of travel, and you're lucky to see your family once a week. Ask yourself what you can change so that you can enjoy spending time with your family.

Remember: make happiness a priority. Here's how.

Step One: Identify what is wrong in your present situation. Take time to really evaluate what occurs in your life and what you want to change about it. If it's not working, then maybe it's time to toss it! By identifying the areas in your life that you would like to change, you are taking the first step toward stepping out of your comfort zone. (You are changing your perspective so that you can change your reality.) It might be hard, and it might be exhausting, but your hard work will pay off—if you keep persevering. Keep in mind that the thing not working in your life may not immediately be obvious. It may be a specific person poisoning the environment; it may be a particular location; it may even be you. Remember to be brutally honest with yourself.

Step Two: Keep on trying even when the going gets tough. This may mean you have to reevaluate your circumstances and enact changes. Not everything is going to work out the way you want it to the first time. The biggest mistake you can make is to give up when something doesn't work the first time. Many successful people didn't succeed the first time. The factor that ensured their success was perseverance, even when their task felt impossible.

Know where you are in your life and picture where you would like to go. Push aside self-doubt and past failures; both of these are harmful to success. No one has become successful by discouraging him- or herself. Don't fall into this trap.

Keyword:

> **Change:** the active state of turning your new perspective into your new reality. This usually involves stepping out of your comfort zone.

Getting to Know Yourself

By the time they've graduated from college, most people have some idea of personality science. Personality science, in basic terms, is learning what makes you tick, what makes you, you. There are several camps of ideas that most psychologists fall under, and each one of these camps has a test.

If you want to get to know yourself better, I can't think of anything better than taking one or all of these tests. Each personality type approaches success and setbacks in a different way that can affect, or even sabotage, your attempts to follow your dreams. So before we even start visualizing your dreams in the next chapter, let's delve into the field of personality science.

Top Three Tests:

1. Myers-Briggs

   This test and theory are based on Carl Jung's teaching. It is a test designed by a mother/daughter team and is one of the easiest tests to share with othersdue to its unique, and often telling, four-letter formula. Due to its easy sharing ability, it is extremely popular in business and pop culture. While this four-letter personality combinatio, one of sixtee, is easy, sometimes it is limited due to its rigid format, and we all know that no one acts the same way all the time. For instance, my editor behaves like an INTJ, but at work in her business she is an ENTJ, and with her husband and children she shifts to an INFJ. I myself switch around as well.

   The Myers-Briggs test checks your personality characteristics in four separate areas: Extroversion/Introversion, iNtuition/Sensing, Thinking/Feeling, and Judging/Perceiving. To take the test, you can follow the link here: https://www.16personalities.com/free-personality-test

2. Big 5

   The Big 5 is the personality test that most psychologists use these days, partly because it views human personality on a continuum rather than a simple "this or that" like the Myers-Briggs.

It also tests you on five different aspects of your personality rather than four, though there are some Myers-Briggs tests that now incorporate this fifth elemen as well, which is called neuroticism. I generally call it your confidence meter.

3. DISC

DISC is by far the simplest test and gives you a good idea of what the driving force behind your motives is. DISC stands fo Dominance, Steadiness, Conscientiousness, and Influence.

The Habit Factor

Did you know that people have distinct habit-forming personalities as well? In addition to your personality, your habits have personality preferences as well. According to Gretchen Rubin in her book *Better than Before*, there are four different habit-formation types. Follow the link here to find a simple test to find out yours. If you want to know more about habit formation, which is handy to have in goal setting, which we'll discuss later, follow this link: https://www.16personalities.com/free-personality-test.

Final Thoughts

It is important to note that there are no negative personalities. To each personality type there are negatives and positives. The Myers-Briggs or the Big 5 can't tell you your moral alignment. Certain personality types make nice villains in stories, but in real life, they are quite kind and moral people. So if you happen to find yourself in Lord Voldemort's shoes as an INTJ or Darth Vader's as an ESTJ, or are someone with a high level of neuroticism or a low level of agreeableness, just remember it takes all kinds of people to make the world run smoothly.

Here we're only concerned with getting to know who you are and accepting that. You can work on improving areas you find lacking later in this book.

12

If you feel the need for more information or research on the topic (perhaps you INTPs . . .), you can check out the websites we've already talked about or read a few interesting books on the topic, such as *Type Talk*.

Looking on the Bright Sid

Before I end this chapter, I'll try to leave you with a few positive thoughts. One of the best ways to achieve the change you need and improve your life is to start your own business, one that helps you follow your purpose in life. Before you do that, though, you need to understand one more thing:

If you are serious about monetizing your passion, there is *no room for regrets*. Leave the past behind and move forward. Accept who you are and where you are now. At this very moment. Most of us could sit and think of two hundred things we should have done differently in life. I know I sure can, but I also know doing that isn't helpful. So say goodbye to "should-haves."

When I was twenty-six years old, I discovered the world of government contracting. At that point in time, I was afraid of EVERYTHING! I had never flown before, and now not only was I about to get on a plane for the first time to meet my employer for processing, but I was also facing a fourteen-hour plane ride to Dubai. During my tenure as a contractor, I made a significant amount of money, even though I didn't initially make the best financial decisions. At the end of my contracting endeavor, I realized that even though I wasn't a millionaire, I had accomplished more than I had set out to do. For instance, I was able to eliminate old debt, something that enabled me to pursue my dream of purchasing my first home. I was able to fund my education, enhance my savings, and assist family and friends who were in need. And lastly, I was able to start many successful businesses.

Even though I made some bad choices during my time abroad, I made tremendous progress in my life and was able to blossom into adulthood. For a while after that, I often thought, "If only I had learned about contracting a bit sooner, I could have retired early or saved more money." Now I remember that I have a great life despite its sporadic flaws. Occasionally, I am totally amazed with myself. I remember watching a clip of myself speaking to an audience for the very first time. I thought to myself: "Wow, that's me. That's me up there saying all those empowering things!"

Realizing that life is as it should be is refreshing. No, I didn't grow up to be a psychiatrist as I had planned, but I'm happy. I'm not a millionaire, but I'm happy. I don't own a mansion, but my home is one of the most peaceful and loving places on Earth. And I'm happy.

See what happens when you decide to look on the bright side? See what happens when you accept your current state and bask in the ambiance of being thankful for where you've been, where you are, and where you are going? How exciting! Know how amazing you really are.

Are you ready to start looking forward instead of backward? We're not time travelers, and no one can change what has happened in the past, but you can certainly learn valuable lessons that will contribute to your success. Dwelling on what could have been does not prepare you for encouraging things to happen. Have you ever tried walking backward? You can't get too far without tripping! The same can be said about looking into your past. If you try it, you will constantly trip on regrets and should-have-beens and never accomplish your dreams.

I encourage you to walk forward, to leave your past behind. Take the lessons you have learned and apply them. Life experiences are meant to be learned from, not dwelt upon and regretted. If you live with past regrets, then you have no hope of having a successful future. Take your knowledge, your experience, and your insight and use them for what lies before you right now. Don't be afraid to leave your past behind!

You may not be able to get rid of your regrets at the snap of your fingers. Don't worry and don't feel guilty; it's not always possible to control your thoughts and feelings. But by focusing on the positive instead of the negative, you have taken the first step to getting rid of your regrets, doubts, and guilt. Try this: every time you think something negative about yourself, think something positive immediately after. Every time someone says something negative about you, say something positive about yourself—and about them. This sort of active positive thinking is a choice, and it's a choice everyone can make.

Here are a few good rules for life:

- Choose to be happy. Don't blame others for your unhappiness.

- Choose to take care of yourself. Don't blame others for what you don't have.

- Choose to keep going. Don't blame others for your road blocks.

- Choose to accept who you are. Don't blame the past for your present.

- You can be whatever you choose to be. And yes, you may blame (or thank!) yourself for that.

ACTION DIARY:

Date: _____

Pick three regrets you acknowledge often:

What are some things you could have done differently to change these regrets into success?

Now name the positive things that have come from accepting your regrets and/or the instances when things didn't go as you'd planned:

Now that you've acknowledged your regrets and accepted their outcomes, how can you improve your perception of change?

Chapter 2
The Connection

Vision

Even the smallest of things begins with a vision. A thought about someone, something, or doing something . . . becomes something real. You are no exception to this. Before you can achieve, you need to know *what* to achieve, and that's where visualization enters the picture.

Example:

> When we pick out clothes for the next morning, we are preparing our minds for what we would like to *see* ourselves look like. We think about what we want to wear, we rummage through our closet, and then we hold the chosen outfit against our body in the best mirror we have in our house. Then we decide. We decide how our face looks. We decide how our hair looks.

Every day, we make decisions based on what we have consciously decided to do for that day, the next day, the next moment. Sometimes, we make a decision about what is going to happen next year on a specific date (e.g., a vacation or a wedding). The list goes on and on, but what remains the same is simple: *We visualize an intention or thought to bring about a specific outcome.* So it follows that the first step to achieving the outcome we want is to visualize it.

What have you visualized today? Has it come true?

Some may say that this type of thinking requires too many expectations. In my experience, however, this type of thinking enables energy—energy that will inevitably bring desires into reality. Visualizing that end result becomes the motivation that enables you to achieve that end result.

Keyword:

> **Visualization:** a technique in which you imagine your future self achieving your goals in order to eaccomplish a specific outcome. This mental exercise helps give you the initial energy needed to follow your passion. Visualization alone is not enough for success; it must be followed by action. However, it is the important first step you need to take.

Passion

Visualization and energy start with one thing: passion. Without passion, dreams are unattainable. Have you ever had a dream without passion? Probably not, and for good reason, since passion is what drives you toward your dream.

A number of things can and will get in the way of you achieving your dreams, if you let them. Doubt, fear, worry, and lack of purpose are factors that can inhibit your vision and prevent it from becoming reality. Instead of getting bogged down by negative influences, focus on the reason for your passion and use that reason to drive you to the next step.

Your passion is your fuel. To drive yourself forward, you must know what drives your motivation. There are different ways to accomplish staying motivated. Here are a few:

- Keep up your motivation with methods of your own.

- Journal or get assistance from a mentor or coach.

- Utilize goal setting to have tangible proof of progress.

- Remember that you are your own best critic.

- Every single day, take the time you need to encourage yourself and the behaviors you want to hold onto—and keep your motivation driving forward!

Keyword:

> **Passion:** your fuel. It is the thing you are really good at and really love, and it drives you forward. Passion creates a motivation feedback loop: you want to do something, you achieve that thing, which in turn gives you the motivation to do the next thing. This is an efficient (and sometimes addictive!) cycle!

Goals, Momentum, and Focus

What you want in life isn't simply handed to you. You must put forth effort to achieve it. Take that extra step to figure out what motivates you, and then work as hard as you can to keep that motivation alive. Set small goals. Set big ones. Do whatever it takes to channel your motivation into your daily life. We'll move into more specific ways to work on goal setting in a moment. When you have gained the necessary motivation, the rest will start to fall into place. Keep in mind that motivation may not come easily. Be ready to work hard for what you want. Be ready to achieve.

Once you've gained the motivation to keep your passions alive, you will see a measurable difference in how you handle your day-to-day routines. Many people give up too easily in the mistaken belief that their passions and dreams are impossible. Life wasn't meant to be easy; sometimes, you have to work harder than you think you ought to in order to achieve what you want. Take a look at successful people. Observe their backgrounds. Most of them didn't come by success easily. Ease is not nature's way. Hard work will pay off.

To achieve success, you just have to want it badly enough. Do you?

Motivation needs both momentum and focus. When you generate enough momentum to get going, your subconscious automatically produces enough energy to maintain and/or increase your speed.

Example:

> Imagine that you're a kid again. You're riding your bike around the neighborhood. While on your usual path, you've reached the exciting hill that you and your buddies love. You anxiously begin to pedal faster. Though your thighs and knees are aching, you persevere with determination and anticipation. Finally, you arrive on top of the hill. You smile at your accomplishment, and there you go! Down the hill, full speed ahead! Your bike is moving so quickly that you can barely keep your feet on the pedals. You reach the bottom of the hill, but you're still moving quickly because of all the momentum you've created. Your hair is flying in the wind, and you're riding down the street thinking about how much fun you're having and how you can't wait to do it again. Feels good, right?

Momentum. When you create the momentum necessary to pursue your dreams, you tend to look forward to the hills you hit along your path. You jump for joy at any sign of an incline in the road. You anticipate the effort necessary, and you pedal forth in pursuit. The reward pays off.

Keyword:

> **Motivation:** a combination of momentum and focus. It is what keeps you going—what keeps you fulfilling your purpose by pursuing your passion.

Finding Your Purpose

It's often said that it's easier to visualize things when you have a purpose (that is, when you intend to fulfill and engage in your passion). Have you ever sat down and wondered about your purpose in life? Have you ever wondered if you were in the right place doing the right thing? Have you ever pondered your ideal place in life only to realize you had no idea where that was? If so, that's okay. Don't worry. You're not the only one.

Finding your purpose in life can be quite challenging. Your purpose is a trait that excites you and gives you responsibility. Responsibility? You feel responsible for sharing your passion with the world and allowing the energy from it to continuously lead you to prosperous decisions in your life. Your purpose is to fulfill your passion. Your passion is that thing you're really good at. It's that thing that can make any bad day into a good day. It's that thing that you love doing no matter what.

Do you have a powerful purpose that drives you forward? Is there a magical gleam in your eyes when you consider it? Do you have the desire to make it? If you answered with anything but a "yes," then you have not found your true purpose and the work you put into your false one will be futile. Search deeper for the purpose that lights a spark in you. Your desire for your purpose must be strong. Don't settle for less.

Rest assured that you absolutely do not need to be frightened to dream a huge dream. To keep smaller goals in mind, you must see large, bold goals. Having only small goals is not enough.

Have you ever imagined that passion is like fuel for an engine? Without a reason that's big enough, you'll have difficulty making your passion happen—which means you'll have difficulty fulfilling your purpose. Your engine will run out of steam. Find your passion to help drive and motivate you, and you'll find your purpose. When you have a real purpose, failure is no longer an option: your purpose takes over and does the driving while you enjoy the view.

Every person on this planet has a purpose. Most haven't searched for their purpose and ultimately live their lives floundering, trying to make it through. Do you know what your purpose is? If not, don't worry. Some people cannot identify a clear purpose for themselves. Take some time and ask yourself a few questions that will lead you to your purpose:

- What do you enjoy doing?

- What are you good at?

- What are your natural talents?

- What are your strengths and weaknesses?

Work with that at which you excel. Ultimately, you will be able to find your purpose by looking deep within yourself.

In the previous chapter, we discussed change and getting outside your comfort zone. This too is essential in finding your life purpose. You need to break outside of your shell. By talking, listening, and watching others you will get a better sense of both the "big picture" and yourself. It's important to have this different view, to be able to see others and see yourself as others see you. This experience will give you a better understanding of yourself and others, which in turn will help you find that life purpose. Nobody finds their purpose (or becomes successful) alone, so be prepared to learn from others.

But also be prepared to learn from yourself. As the great Parker Palmer says: "Before I can tell my life what I want to do with it, I need to listen to my life tell me who I am." Look at your past, your history, and try to identify common patterns and themes running through what you have experienced. How do these themes relate to what you love to do? How do they prevent you from doing what you want to do?

Look at the world around you. Every great person has had a vision in his or her life. Even those you may never have heard of have risen above their life circumstances by being focused and passion-driven. Don't put your dreams on the shelf simply because you think you lack the time to visualize what you want from your life or your business. Make the time. Every success story started with a dream and a purpose. Those who achieved success had enough passion, motivation, and desire to turn dreams into realities. The only person you're harming by not pursuing and visualizing your dreams and goals is yourself.

Take the time and effort necessary to build your purpose into a success. The only person who can make this happen is you. Talking about it is one thing. In order for your purpose to become useful, you must act on it and shape it into what you want and need it to be. A vision is nothing without action. Just keep that in mind as you keep on dreaming. Action is your key to achievement!

Do you have what it takes to make your dreams and passions into realities? Of course you do! It takes time, focus, and effort to make that dream a living thing. Breathe life into your passion. Find your purpose and let it become your passion and your life. It may not be easy, but in the end, it will be worth it. Remember the metaphor of going uphill on your bike. The ride down is your reward.

Keywords:

> **Dreams:** your huge, overarching, or ultimate goals. Dreams do not have to be finite; they can be an ongoing process.

> **Goals:** stepping stones or achievements that contribute to fulfilling your purpose. Setting both small, reasonable goals and large, overarching goals ("dreams") can help motivate you.

> **Purpose:** your purpose is to pursue your passion. This pursuit will include many small goals and one or more dreams.

Granting Yourself Permission

Deciding to pursue your innermost passions can be scary. As an individual, you must commit and put everything you have into making it your reality. You must want it. It may not be comfortable or easy. You must be prepared for that when you begin your journey.

Life is tough. The path is rocky (but beautiful). There will always be someone or something there to discourage you from taking your passions and desires to the next level. Living safely will ensure safety but will not ensure happiness. True happiness comes from living out what you were meant to live out. Don't set yourself back based on what others might think or feel.

The only person who can make your dreams and passions come true is you. If you wait for someone else's approval, you are setting yourself back from accomplishing what you want and are meant to do. Don't be afraid to give yourself the permission to succeed. Give yourself all the permission required to dream and transform your purpose and passions into a living reality!

Picking your Main Goals

Now that you've had a great pep talk about passion, motivation, and visualization, it's time to talk about your specific goals.

Setting yourself goals is important. Goals tell you where you want to be, and more importantly having a goal is motivation in and of itself. Simply having something to aim for is enough to give you the drive to get there in the end. And goals are a great way of measuring your progress. It's a human truth that we all need to achieve in order to stay motivated, and goals allow us to "check things off the list." Achieving goals means measurable progress. But how do we go about choosing those main goals?

Firstly, you might want to think about which broad categories your goals might lie in. You may, of course, have goals that lie in more than one category. Here are the main categories you should think about:

- **Career:** Perhaps you want to run your own ad agency, maybe become an independent worker, rather than an employee.

- **Financial:** Perhaps you want a great retirement fund, or to buy a home.

- **Education:** Perhaps you want a higher-level degree, or a degree or training in a completely different field.

- **Physical:** Perhaps you want to lose weight, or run a marathon!

- **Family:** Perhaps you want to marry or divorce, or have children.

- **Community:** Perhaps you want to change the world in some way, or make your neighborhood a better place to live.

Yes, some of these goals aren't business related, but don't worry about that for now. You never know when business and pleasure or business and family or business and community might intersect. Your life goal may well end up being something you never even considered as a business, so it's important that you don't only focus on the career goal at this point.

Now take a piece of paper and write down as many of the above headings as you're interested in (feel free to add more if you'd like) and begin brainstorming beneath each heading. Brainstorming simply means you write down anything that comes into your head when you think about each of the categories you've chosen. There are no bad ideas, no ideas too crazy or impossible, and no judgment. Just allow yourself free rein to write anything you wish. Spend at least half an hour doing this, and the longer, the better!

When you're satisfied that you're done brainstorming, walk away. Leave that paper for a day or two, or even a week. When you're finally ready to come back to it, start looking at the ideas you have written down. Pick out the things that really speak to you, the goals that are really important to you. Eventually, you should have a list of several things that will become your main goals in life. Don't worry at this point about achievability; there's plenty of time for that later!

The goals that you choose should be SMART goals. SMART is an acronym that's very useful when working with goal setting:

- **Specific:** A goal should state exactly what you want to do in as specific a way as possible ("Write a book about how to change your career" is better than "Write a book").

- **Measurable:** Goals should be as measurable as possible ("Get 500 more readers for my blog this month" is better than "Get more readers for my blog").

- **Actionable:** Goals should contain "action" verbs (go, walk, write, do), rather than "being" verbs ("Talk to 3 new people every day" is better than "Be more sociable").

- **Realistic:** This is a tough one, but goals should be somewhat realistic, though don't limit yourself too much. We all know that "becoming invisible" isn't a realistic goal, though "getting a PhD in biology" is something that's realistic, though it might be difficult.

- **Time-Bound:** Finally, as far as possible, goals should be time-bound; there should be a time limit involved ("Start a new website by the end of January" is better than "Start a new website").

Once you have around five or so main goals, you can then move on to the next step!

Setting up your Main Goals

Life is tough. The path is rocky (but beautiful). There will always be someone or something there to discourage you from taking your passions and desires to the next level. Living safely will ensure safey, but will not ensure happiness. True happiness comes from living out what you were meant to live out. Don't set yourself back based on what others might think or feel.

Setting your big goals is only the first part of the process in goal setting. If you thought big in the last section like I encouraged you, then you should have this impossible-looking, hard goal in front of you and you should be thinking, "But how is this going to happen?" Chill. Relax. Take a quick breather. The Bible was written over 5,000 years. J.K. Rowling spent the first half of her life creating Harry Potter.

Here we'll help you chew off some bite-sized pieces of your big goal.

The process of simplifying your goals down to more achievable (and less intimidating) tasks is actually quite easy. You have a big goal, one that's, say, a goal for five years from now. You simply take that goal and divide it into pieces, then divide those pieces into pieces, then those pieces of pieces into pieces, and, well, you get the picture. Perhaps a more concrete example would help!

Let's say that your goal is to write a book in a year. You're going to write a big book, a 120,000-word manuscript. Well, that's 12,000 words a month, so there's your first goal. 12,000 words a month is around 3,000 words a week; there's your next goal. 3,000 words a week is 500 words a day (with one day off a week, because detoxing is always important!). In just three lines we've suddenly turned that terrifying 120,000-word behemoth of a book into a much more manageable (and less frightening) 500 words a day.

The above example is a relatively simplified one. But you can use the same basic principle to divide any large goal into something more manageable. You just need a plan of action. Perhaps your goal is to start your own landscaping business. The first thing you need to do is figure out what needs to be done and what timeframe it can be done in. You don't begin with building a landscaping business. You begin with buying a lawnmower!

By breaking large goals down into manageable pieces, you not only avoid becoming so over-awed that you don't dare approach that goal in the first place, but you also give yourself measurable progress toward that large goal. Completing a daily checklist, then a weekly one, then a monthly one, and a yearly one, all come together in the end to accomplish a main goal! Think of your "pieces" as mile markers on that rocky path and you'll understand the satisfaction you'll feel as you steadily approach your destination.

Action Diary:

Date: _____

What are some of your passions?

How does exercising your passion(s) make you feel?

How often do you get to explore your passion(s)?

If not often, why?

Be sure to look back at your responses periodically. This way, you can track your progress.

Chapter 3
The Idea

Being your own boss has its benefits. However, being an entrepreneur and starting your own business can be time-consuming and difficult. The monetary gain from being a successful entrepreneur is something many dream of, but only certain people possess the qualities necessary to achieve. Have you thought about taking the next step? If so, you need to know some of the basic characteristics of a successful entrepreneur. If you don't possess any of these characteristics, don't worry—you can achieve them. Anything is possible with willpower and motivation to succeed! On top of being "mentally" ready to be an entrepreneur, you'll also need a great idea. But that idea might be easier to come up with than you realize!

The Characteristics of an Entrepreneur

Before you jump into the deep pool of business, you need to make sure that you're ready to swim. Being an entrepreneur is very difficult, but it's not impossible. There are certain characteristics many entrepreneurs have in common:

- **Motivation:** We have already discussed motivation in the previous chapter, and being motivated by a passion is a big characteristic of a successful entrepreneur!

- **Flexibility:** If you currently work in an office, then chances are that you have an HR department, an IT department, an accounting department, and so on. If you're an entrepreneur, chances are that at least at the beginning you're going to be fulfilling all these roles yourself. An entrepreneur is flexible and willing to turn his or her hand to different jobs in order to get a business up and running. Fortunately, as long as you're willing to work and learn, this is an easy characteristic to obtain. In today's world, the knowledge you need to fulfill most roles is readily available at the click of a mouse!

- **Risk Taking:** Starting a new business is always a risk—there's the risk of failure, the risk that you'll lose money. But there are also everyday risks: do you risk hiring someone else to do your marketing and paying them only to find out they don't do as you wish? An entrepreneur is not afraid of taking risks and has good judgment when it comes to when to take and when not to take risks. A lot of this comes from experience, and as long as you're willing to risk a certain amount, and willing to fail at least in some things, your ability to judge risks will improve over time. But have no doubt that there WILL be risk involved. Starting a business is not for the fainthearted (or for those who can't afford to lose and start again!).

- **Vision and Drive:** Entrepreneurs have vision and drive. Luckily for you, we've already discussed how to envision your goals and how to motivate yourself to achieve them. Just remember to break down your goals into more manageable actions, and you'll be fine!

- **Open-Mindedness:** A good entrepreneur is open-minded. Things change, businesses change, products change, and customers change. That means you need to constantly change in order to keep up. But if you're passionate about your business, you should be able to keep up with all these changes. Don't get stuck in your ways!

- **Decisive:** As a business owner and entrepreneur, you have to be decisive. There's no time for "wait and see," so you need to be able to make a decision when that decision needs to be made. If you're open-minded and have passion and drive, then you should be able to focus on the long-term goal, meaning you're better able to make short-term decisions that accomplish that goal.

- **Business-Oriented:** Finally, there's no avoiding the issue of being business-oriented. To a certain extent, that means having business knowledge: the skills necessary to run an actual business. However, again, these skills are easily learned if you have Internet access and patience! But there's also the question of being focused and goal-oriented. You have to be willing to put your business first in order to succeed!

Yes, there are characteristics that entrepreneurs share. But you can absolutely nurture these characteristics within yourself. You'll need to be prepared to do some work, but if you're intent on that long-term goal, you should know that that work will pay off.

So now that you're prepared to get on with the job, how do you make a decision as to what exactly you want to do?

There are two basic questions you need to start with:

1. What do you want to do?

2. Is it a business venture or hobby?

Deciding What to Do

The number one thing that you must remember in order to start a successful business is that you need to find a business that reflects who you are and what you're interested in. Passion is one of the keys to success. If you don't believe in what you're pursuing, your business goals will be quickly washed away. Those who have been successful in their pursuits have been successful because their businesses are their number one goals. They truly believe in and put everything they have into making sure their businesses survive.

So where do your passions lie? Take some time and think about what you're really passionate about, what you would stand up for, what you truly love. Next, take a look at how you can turn that passion into something that will make a thriving business. Once your passion and vision intersect, you will be able to picture what you would like to make into a business and how you will do so. You must have passion, willpower, and motivation to turn your dream into a successful business. There will be difficulties along the way. No one succeeds without finding failure first. If something doesn't work, you'll need to go back and try something else. Giving up when you run into difficulty is a surefire way to extinguish your dream.

When deciding how to choose a business, there can be a lot of uncertainty. We can make money out of anything, but to make a business work we must have a specific vision, as we've already discussed. But choosing a niche can seem intimidating because there are so many creations already out there, owned and run by millions of people. Since this is the case, remember: there is enough money for everyone. You have something unique to offer. It doesn't matter if what you offer is similar to what many other people offer; it can still work.

Sadly, a business may start out successfully but fade over time. That's where the passion factor comes into play. If your business means something to you, then it has a greater chance of survival. Your passion must be the root of your business in order for it to succeed in the long term. Many people who go into business with high expectations are sorely disappointed when their businesses fade. Most of these individuals did not have the motivation they needed. Their passion faded, and so did their business.

What this means for you is that in order for your business to be successful, it must be grounded in your dream (that is, the ultimate goal of your purpose—the ultimate fulfillment of your passion). Taking your dream and making it into a business will improve the odds that your business will continue to be successful. You believe in your dream so strongly that you will fight whatever comes in order to ensure its success. For instance, you might come up with new marketing techniques and continually improve your product and/ or service. Taking ownership of the intentions you have for your service is somewhat like technology: keep updating yourself and your customers, and you will remain an expert. As time goes on, your business will only get better, because you are keeping up with the needs of the customer.

You must be secure and comfortable with your ideas and dreams before you begin. Starting a business takes a lot of time, effort, and resources. If you jump in blindly, you will more than likely drown in details. Take the time to really think your idea through and know what you're getting into—and how you're going to succeed.

Don't waste your talents and resources on blind faith; most businesses take a lot of planning and work in order to survive. If you want your business to be successful, you must be prepared to give it whatever you have, and you must make sure you know what lies ahead of you.

Business Venture vs. Hobby

Are you confused as to where to begin? Think about what you enjoy doing in your spare time.

What is that one activity you gravitate toward time after time? That is something in which you are most interested and more than likely have a passion for. What can you do to make it a viable business?

Turning a hobby into a business is one of the most common ways of beginning a business. This is simply because you are likely to be enthused about a hobby, so it's far easier to motivate yourself. Plus, of course, if you already do something as a hobby, you already possess some of the expertise you'll need in order to turn that hobby into a business. It's far easier to come up with ideas connected to something you know than to something you know nothing about!

But first, you must realize the difference between a business venture and a hobby. Sure, hobbies can easily become business ventures; however, there is a drastic difference between the two.

Examples:

> Hobby: Suzy crochets scarves for her family. Someone sees one and asks her to make one for them. This person pays

Suzy for her work. She makes money from her hobby, but it is still a hobby, not a business venture.

Business venture: Suzy opens up her own shop on Etsy® and begins to custom-make her scarves. She gains many customers and has a steady income from her shop. She has now entered a business venture because she is using her hobby as one of her primary sources of income.

A hobby is something you really enjoy doing in your free time. Almost anything can be considered a hobby—riding a bicycle, fixing a car, etc. However, doing these things does not guarantee an income. They're just things you enjoy and invest your time in on a regular basis. A business venture is something that makes a sustainable income and a profit. For example, instead of fixing up cars for fun (hobby) you buy and fix cars to resell with the intention of making money from the finished product (business venture).

In both cases, you are engaging in an activity and making something useful. You tend to be passionate about your hobbies, so why not make a business from your hobbies? The passion you have to see your hobby succeed could be the driving force you need in order to run a successful business!

The Pros and Cons and How to Turn a Hobby into a Business

There are both pros and cons when it comes to turning your hobby into a business. The pros are simple: you may end up with a profitable business doing something you truly love, you already possess much of the knowledge you may need in your chosen area, and you're already passionate about your hobby. But what about the cons? The main downside here is that you may be taking something you love and enjoy and turning it into work. There is always the risk that you will stop enjoying your hobby because it has now become your job. But a successful entrepreneur is a risk taker, and this is a risk that is usually worth it since the pros of making this decision outweigh the cons.

Of course, we're going to go into a lot more detail about how to go about monetizing your hobby, but there are some general points you'll want to keep in mind before continuing:

- **Self-Assessment is Key:** You'll need to continuously self-assess in this process, and at the beginning you must be aware that it will take time, effort, and money to build a business from your hobby. Is this something you're honestly willing to do?

- **The Whole Hog or Not?:** While it's true that you'll need plenty of time and money to begin a business, it's also true that many people begin a business as a side job, rather than as a main job. You'll need to decide whether you need to keep working a regular job (and therefore earn more money but have less time) alongside starting your business.

- **Network, Network, Network:** Just as with any job or business, networking is going to be key. And this is true even before beginning your business. Don't be afraid to reach out to friends, family, colleagues, even other blog writers and experts to get feedback and ideas, and to find out whether your idea has a market or not.

- **The Uniqueness Factor:** You don't have to come up with an idea or product that's completely unique; in fact, you almost certainly won't. What you will need to do is find a unique viewpoint or service, or a unique pricing method, or a unique set of expertise, or *something* unique that makes your service stand out. This could be as simple as offering 30-minute personal training sessions for the busy client, rather than the standard 60-minute sessions. Or updating your blog daily rather than weekly. Or offering your crocheted scarves in color mixtures that aren't otherwise available. There is enough money out there for everyone, but small businesses can find it difficult to compete for customers. Making yourself a little unique is important.

- **Resources:** There are plenty of resources available to help you; all you need to do is look for them. You've already made a great start with this book! But don't be daunted by things such as taxes or how to format your Kindle book or any of the other details. Free resources abound; look for help, and you will find it!

What are your hobbies? Could they become successful businesses? Why not let your interest be the force behind starting your own business? Take the time and think about this. If you're less than passionate about your day job, why not take something you are passionate about and make it into a business? Wouldn't it be great to enjoy your job?

Think about the possibilities and see how your passion can also be your business!

Keywords:

Hobby: an activity pursued for its own sake or for fun. A hobby will not provide you with a significant source of income. Hobbies are done in your free time.

Business Venture: an activity pursued for the sake of money. A business venture provides you with a significant portion of your income. Business ventures are pursued during your work time. A business venture may grow out of a hobby.

ACTION DIARY:

Date: _____

What are four hobbies that you enjoy?

Have you ever thought about turning one of the hobbies into a business? If so, why and which one?

What has prevented you from moving forward in this business endeavor?

What do you feel that you can offer customers by turning your hobby into a business?

Section Two

Strategize

Chapter 4
Do the Research

After evaluating your interests and potential business ideas, and finding an idea you think could make a profitable and fulfilling business . . . comes the hard work. A dream can stay a dream forever. In order for it to become something that works, you must put in time and effort. This takes research and strategizing. In this section, I'm going to offer some suggestions and resources to help you figure out how your dream can and will become a reality.

Note: These steps depend on YOU and how much time and effort you're willing to invest.

Some plans that sound great on paper won't work in the real world, and that's okay. You took the time and the effort to research your niche and found out that the way you planned on implementing your dream wasn't necessarily feasible. If you ran in blindly, you risked losing your hard-earned time and money. If you took the time to do your research and track where your ideas were heading, you saved yourself a lot of hardship. Failing at this point means you've lost some time. Failing at a later date could mean losing your time and your savings!

Even if your initial business ideas aren't feasible, there are avenues you can take in order to come up with a business plan that will be both fulfilling and successful. It's rare that a first product idea, or even a second, is successful. Ever heard of Traf-O-Data? Not many people have, but the creator of this company later became the richest man in the world (it was Bill Gates' first company!). Use your tools, take your time, and know what you're getting into. If you go into this knowing what to expect, then you will be better prepared for the challenges your business encounters . . . and better prepared for the successes.

Research is Necessary

Now that you've discovered your product, it's time to do research. Yeah, I know: research is boring, and it seems to take forever! However, in order to be prepared for your new business venture, you must know what to expect and have a plan. As I mentioned in the previous section, if you have no clear direction, then your business is doomed from the beginning. If you want to make your dream a reality, get started on the right foot.

Understand your niche. In order to get a valid, overall picture of what you must do in order to make your business go in the right direction, you need to look for products, manufacturers, sellers, affiliates, and other relative resources inside your chosen niche. Not all of these factors are going to apply to your goods or services, but for those areas that do, you need to be well informed and up to date. Read blogs, read product reviews and consumer reports, read appropriate trade magazines, and read biographies of people who did the same thing you want to do. The information is out there if you search for it.

Know your market. What factors about this market make your product and/or service in demand? By researching your market and knowing pros and cons, you will be able to figure out the best way to introduce your business to the world. Is your business still just a little idea that you've pondered for months or even years? By doing your market research, you will be able to understand the economic aspects of what your business entails. This includes income and expenses. Unfortunately, some people do not look at such factors and end up failing because their costs outweigh their profits. Deciding to make a widget that costs you $4 to produce and that market research says can be sold at a $3 price point obviously makes no sense. And yet you'd be surprised how many people fall into this trap. Knowing your market means knowing all the ins and outs. It's all very well to create a high-end restaurant in your local area where there's no competition, but are people in your area able and willing to pay high-end prices?!

Know what to expect. By knowing your market and knowing where you want your business to lead, you are setting yourself up for success. I mentioned before that many businesses fail after about the third year. That is a discouraging statistic, but if you're aware of the risks and the costs, you stand a better chance of defying this statistic. Know what success in business will take and know what to expect. These two things will help you when you face the successes and the challenges your business will bring.

Familiarize yourself with similar products. Take some time to see how similar products or services are marketed. Ask yourself:

- What are some things that make this product/service attractive to buyers?

- Does this product use marketing strategies I can use or improve upon?

The Internet provides a wealth of information at your fingertips. Don't be afraid to use it. Learn from the successes and failures of others. This will help you foresee difficulties in your journey.

Research doesn't necessarily have to be books and boring statistics. There are some other options:

- Purchase a similar product to the one you plan to market to see how it's packaged and how it works.

- Check out how the product is rated and read remarks from customers. Make notes on customer suggestions (and on your own thoughts) about how to improve the product.

Taking time to research what your product can offer that the competitors' do not will help you create a product that's one step ahead. It will also help you have that unique edge we mentioned in the previous chapter that will make your product or service more desirable than your competitors'. By reading customer discussions, you can offer a product or service that consumers want.

There are many ways to learn about the markets and how items sell, and all of them can better prepare you for venturing out on your own. The marketing world can be scary, but it can also be rewarding. Again, though, by being open-minded and willing to learn, and by spending time familiarizing yourself with the language used and the main players and products in your niche, you'll get there in the end. There's really nothing to be afraid of; everyone else started out at some point in the same position that you're in!

Keyword Research

While doing your search, be sure to take note of the phrases you use in your search engine. Be sure to use common phrases as well as descriptive phrases. The key to describing your product is to capitalize on attractive and informative keywords. Think about a time when you were looking for a specific product that could fulfill a specific need. You had no idea of what it was called, but you knew what it did, what it looked like, and even where you could find it in stores. Using this information, you were able to find it on the Internet. That is what we call "keyword research," and it is a powerful marketing resource.

Keyword research is a great way to see how items are described and marketed. By typing in keywords that describe the product, you will be able to find exactly what you're looking for. Before you try keyword research on a product, try it on an activity or hobby.

Example:

> I'm really into reading. Just yesterday, I saw a commercial on television that advertised a product I could download that would enable me to read all of my favorite books without ever having to go out to a bookstore. The download would be almost instantaneous, and I could read the book in a matter of minutes. However, I could not remember

what the ad called this product. This is where keyword research can help me find what I'm looking for.

First, I remembered the product was described as an e-reader. That was, therefore, the first search I performed. When I typed in "e-reader," I got a list of products by every electronics manufacturer on the planet. Then I remembered that the product was brightly colored like a television, so, to narrow my search, I added the keyword "backlit." This helped, but it wasn't enough, so I added another keyword—the name of the manufacturer. This really narrowed it down. I saw the product I wanted within the first few pages of my search results!

Keyword research can help you determine the characteristics of other competing products, which will give you an edge when determining the specifications of your own product. Maybe your product could be a great mix of two similar products!

All successful products market their features by using keywords that will help the consumers find them. When you're researching keywords that describe your product or service, think about how others will be searching for it. Be as descriptive as possible to make your product pop up on keyword searches more often!

Most people shop online nowadays, and keywords are an important part of how they find the products and services they look for. Keep this in mind as you prepare to market your business. Remember: make your product something you would want to buy, and make it easy to find!

Keyword:

Keyword Research: the practice used to optimize results in a search engine. By choosing attractive and informative keywords to describe your product, you can make that product easier for potential customers to find.

Practical Tip: Keyword Research

If you're struggling with the concept of keywords and find it difficult to come up with different search terms, then there's an easy way to get lots of options. Google has an advertising program known as AdWords, and it's simple to leverage this into doing some of the keyword research for you. Though AdWords is designed for paying advertisers, you can freely use the program to find keywords related to your ideas. Don't worry about the pricing index and numbers you see, and you won't need to pay anything. All you need to concern yourself with is the ideas that the program produces.

Simply go to https://adwords.google.com and log in using your normal Google account information. Under the Tools tab find "keyword planner" and then select "search for new keywords using a phrase, website, or category." You can then put in some of the keywords you've already found and find which other keywords are connected to those you've chosen. This takes five minutes and is an easy way to find lots of search terms related to the kind of product or service you're thinking of providing!

It can also be a valuable way of researching what consumers are interested in. If "widget black" gets a lot more average monthly searches than "widget red" then you might want to consider only producing black widgets!

Domain Names

This brings up another facet of research that you need to consider. While doing your keyword searches, try typing in the domain names relevant to your niche. See what's already out there, and see what's available. Having the right domain name is important when trying to market your product or service. Make a list of catchy domain names that are not already taken. This will make it easy for you to decide on a catchy name and domain for your business.

Keyword:

> **Domain Name**: a way of identifying a group of associated web pages. For example, all web pages within a specific

website will have the same domain name. In many cases, websites have domain names easily associated with the names of their websites. For example, the domain name of the website Amazon is amazon.com.

You can brainstorm website ideas as well as using your keyword research to come up with good names too. An easy-to-remember product and website name is a great start to making people aware of who you are and what you do.

Experiment with Other Products

If you're thinking of creating a product for your niche, you must at some point become a consumer to your competitors. That's right; it's time to shop! Buy products that are doing well in your niche. Becoming the subject-matter expert in your niche is the only way to stay ahead of your competitors—which means that even if you know one half of a percent more than they do, you are the subject-matter expert. What better way to become an expert than to familiarize yourself with products that are already on the market and generating revenue? Give it a try!

For starters, let's say for instance your niche is fitness and your focus is CrossFit® training. You love to do CrossFit® (i.e., you have *passion* for it), and you want to find out more information on how to enhance your endurance and skillset. You do keyword research to find more information about CrossFit®. While doing so, you find that the fitness niche is massive and has a world of areas for concentration. Go through and pick a product with great reviews and preferably a lot of videos. Remember, this product should spark your interest and be affordable. Not all products will be free, so spend wisely. After all, this is part of your business investment. Products to look for would be membership sites, e-books, instructional videos, and freebies. Also, sign up for affiliate information if it is available and you have the time. We will talk about affiliate businesses in the upcoming chapters.

Many shopping sites (particularly Amazon) allow you to sort products in a niche by popularity as well as by customer reviews, so make sure to note how popular and how well-rated different products are when making your purchasing decision. Remember: you're a customer right now, and you're deciding on a product in the same way that *your* customers will one day decide to buy your product!

This is where your research comes in. Pick some products that peak and use them. While using them, make notes about the products, both positive and negative. The goal is to capitalize on the good *and* the bad. Choose to like the good things about the product because those good things are usually the reason people expend their cash and time on them. Choose to appreciate the bad things about the product because they will help you make your product better. Remember: the goal is to offer buyers something they don't have already along with the things they do. Customer satisfaction is obviously important, and it makes the difference between a customer who becomes a repeat customer and one who doesn't, as well as between a customer who recommends you to others and one who doesn't.

Research might not always be the most interesting part of starting a business, but it is what starts your business off on the right foot. Jumping into the business pool after a few swimming lessons is far preferable to jumping in just hoping that you know how to swim. Take your time, do your research, and improve your chances for success!

Action Diary:

Date: _____

Write down your niche ideas (e.g. fitness, cooking, football):

What are some keyword phrases you use to research this niche?

Name a few products that have caught your interest; then buy them:

List pros and cons about each product:

Chapter 5
What Business Structure is Right for You?

In order to set up and run a successful business, you must be able to understand different business types and how they operate. Not understanding business types is like trying to find your way in the dark when it comes to setting up your business. We all know how stumbling in the dark usually ends: you come out with stubbed toes, bruises, and maybe even a few scrapes. It's frustrating and not necessarily fun or exciting. The result can be the same when trying to start a business without knowing where it falls in the business world. Different business types have different pros and cons, as well as different legal processes for setting up, dissolving, and even filing taxes.

This chapter will cover the different types of business entities and how they operate. Remember, the more you understand, the greater your chances are of succeeding!

Most Common Business Entities

There are several types of business structure. If you assume you have a business simply because you've decided your business name, then you are mistaken. Having a vision is good, but knowing where it will take you is a totally different ballgame! It's important that you choose the right form of business structure for your budding company. Even from the very beginning, there will be differences in how different forms of business are set up, the paperwork required, and all kinds of other things. Knowing what type of business you're starting *before* you begin means you'll be able to focus on researching the correct information for your chosen structure (and not waste time learning more "general" things, or rules that won't apply to the kind of company you want to set up).

To get the most out of your new business, you must choose the right type of structure. Selecting the right structure helps maximize your chances of financial and operational success.

As mentioned before, you will be spending a lot of time and energy getting your new business off the ground. You'll need to take some time to research each of these entities and figure out where yours fits in. I'll give a brief synopsis to get you started.

Corporation

Corporations are one of the most popular types of business. You see this type of structure when a business is larger and consists of many locations. Look at fast-food chains. Most of these businesses are associated with corporations. A corporation is the most protected way to build a business (i.e., the way that makes it least likely you'll have to suffer personal financial consequences if your business fails). In corporations, liability is separate from the employees and shareholders. This makes things easier for both the business and its employees. In essence, this means that should a corporation fail, then the employees and shareholders won't be paying off the debts (an important consideration when we're talking about multi-billion-dollar companies!).

There are two main types of corporations, C and S corporations.

A **C corporation** is a business entity that can have an unlimited number of shareholders located anywhere in the world. C corporations are taxed on dividends and shares. If you have had personal experience in the stock market, you know that the price of stock depends on how many shares are available and how well the business that produced them is doing. The more stock you have available determines the price of the stock. If you're anything like me, you look for the lower-priced stocks and hope they rise!

An **S Corporation** is similar, but has a limited number of shares. Share ownership is restricted to United States citizens.

Pros. There are many benefits to being a part of a corporation. Corporations have independent legal and tax structures. They maintain a distinct separation between personal and business debts. Shareholders can easily sell shares or leave shares to family members. This type of business has easily transferable ownership. Corporations are very expandable due to their ability to sell stock (and therefore create more money to put back into the company for expansion). After having your business incorporated, you might decide you want to sell or expand. These things become easier because of the corporate structure!

Cons. There are a few disadvantages to a corporation. Corporations are more difficult to get off the ground due to increased paperwork requirements and higher establishing and running costs. States tends to tax corporations more than other business types. Most companies do not begin as corporations (though there are exceptions). Instead they take advantage of the lower setup costs and easier process of beginning a different business structure, and then "incorporate" at a later date (once they've made lots of money!). This means that the process of setting up a corporation isn't necessarily designed with beginners in mind, though, of course, that shouldn't prevent you from setting up a corporation if that's what you feel you need.

Take some time and weigh the pros and cons. You might be taxed more, but a corporation is the most elastic business structure there is!

Example:

> One of the most popular corporation subsets is retail store chains. Most of these stores are operated by a main office and follow the same rules and guidelines. Retail store chains offer people the opportunity to become shareholders, making it possible for them to own a part of the company. When negative news about these stores, such as security

breaches, hits the media, the prices of the company's stock drop, and shareholders take a loss along with the company.

Think about some of the jobs you have had in the past. Have you ever been offered shares in a company based on the fact that you worked for them? If so, your employer was part of a corporation. Take some time to look at the stock market. Notice that the higher-priced shares belong to extremely successful companies. Now, take a moment and visualize your business on that list. Fun thought, right?

Corporations are important in the business world because most people cannot afford to run large-scale businesses on their own. By having the ability to obtain shareholders and not having personal liability, corporations are better able to fund their operations. This makes it more likely that the business vision behind each corporation will succeed!

Limited Liability Company

Another avenue you could pursue is a limited liability company. A limited liability company is an independent legal structure separate from the owner. Owners' personal and business assets are separate, much like in a corporation. You see a lot of small businesses with "LLC" after their names. The LLC means that they are limited liability companies. An LLC is kind of a compromise between being a corporation and being a sole proprietorship company (which we'll discuss below). You don't get shareholders (so no raising money by selling shares, making expansion slightly more difficult). But you do get to offset some risk (since your personal assets are protected, should the LLC fail, then your home, for example, can't be sold to cover the debts). Plus, the setup process and paperwork such as accounting and taxes are easier with an LLC than with a corporation. As with corporations, there are pros and cons to operating a limited liability company.

Pros. Unlike a corporation, a limited liability company is taxed like a sole proprietorship or a partnership, two business types that will be discussed shortly. This makes filing your taxes much easier. Limited liability companies are not taxed as much as corporations, but they still enjoy the freedom of having separated assets. The LLC structure is more flexible than the corporation structure, making it easier to operate LLCs the way their owners deem appropriate. There is no limit to how many owners can be part of the company. Your buddies want a piece of your vision? No problem!

Cons. The downside to a limited liability company is that, since there is no clear outline of the business structure, the owners of the company must come up with one of their own. This flexibility can make it difficult to define goals, boundaries, and other details. Joe wants to run your business a certain way, Bob wants to run it another, and, sadly, you're stuck in the middle. Time to compromise! And since you don't get to sell stock in your company, any expansion will need to be funded either from profits from your company (if you have them!) or by the owners putting in more money.

A few examples of limited liability companies are AOL and many major automobile manufacturers. These companies run on the freedom of limited liability, but are taxed like individuals or sole proprietorships. Small restaurants often run as LLCs.

Limited liability companies are a good route to go if you're interested in running a business on your own or with others, and you don't feel it's appropriate to include your personal assets in your business finances. If your LLC fails, it won't leave you with personal debts.

Another good part of LLCs is that you don't have to please shareholders or try to sell stock. That might make it more difficult to fund your business, but you know that you're doing what you enjoy doing, and you're not being looked at by multiple parties who technically own a piece of your business. More freedom! But remember, that freedom is a double-edged sword. An LLC gives you the freedom to run your business as you see fit. But it also means there's no provided structure, and you'll need to design one yourself to ensure that you don't get stuck with indecision because owner A doesn't agree with owner B. . . .

Sole Proprietorship

In the section above, we touched upon this type of business entity. Just by looking at the name, you can guess what a sole proprietorship might entail. You're in this on your own. A sole proprietorship is when an individual owns and operates his or her business. This means that the company has one owner, no shareholders, and full legal responsibility. Most small businesses run by individuals fall into the category of sole proprietorship. This is simply because it's easier to set up a sole proprietorship, and depending on the business you have in mind, setup costs can be quite low.

Pros. The benefits of a sole proprietorship are the ease of operation and the ability to do as much or as little as you would like. You could say you have a business, print your own business cards, and start work immediately. You file company taxes with your personal taxes. This makes it easier to operate on a daily basis. For beginning business owners this is a big draw, since it's likely you already know how to do many of the bureaucratic tasks that will be involved with your business (such as tax filing, bank account opening, etc.).

Cons. The owner holds full liability for profits and losses and holds liability for all legal actions against the company. If your company fails and has debts, you are personally liable for them. If your company gets sued, you are liable for legal expenses and settlements. You are taking on the entire weight of a company as one person. This can be a real bummer if your business is not successful. And in the worst cases, this can mean that, should your business catastrophically fail, then your home, car, and other assets can be confiscated and sold to pay off your company's debts. Sole proprietorship owners have to be careful not to accrue so much debt in the business that confiscation of personal property becomes a possibility.

Examples of sole proprietorships include many work-at-home businesses, such as freelancers, artists, and pursuers of other small professional trades. Each company is run by an individual who is solely responsible for it. The owners take responsibility for themselves, what they do, and how big or small their businesses end up. A sole proprietorship can easily expand into a different business entity.

Sole proprietorships are a great way to start a business if you're prepared. You must know the risks of financial and legal difficulties and know how to handle such situations. Since you won't have to answer to anyone about the structure of your business, you have more freedom of operation.

While a sole proprietorship may be the easy way to go, really think about the structure of your business. Is it possible that you'll take a significant loss or have the possibility of legal action against the company? If so, you might want to reconsider this type of business entity, because the risks can be quite high.

Partnership

A partnership operates much like a sole proprietorship, except it has more than one owner. Each owner owns a share of the company. Like a sole proprietorship, a partnership is easy to form and operate and has the same disadvantages. If a partner were sued, that partner would take full liability for the lawsuit. If the company took a loss, the partners would take personal losses. Ask yourself the same questions you would ask about a sole proprietorship to make sure that a partnership is the right type of business for you.

There is one small problem associated with a partnership that isn't a problem in a sole proprietorship, however. This is the relationship between the two partners. You may believe your chosen partner to be trustworthy, but he or she may not turn out to be. You may have an argument with your partner, or your partner may choose to give up his or her share of the business. Personal relationships obviously play a more important role in a partnership than in a sole proprietorship, and partnerships DO fail because of in-fighting. Also consider the separation of the company. A partnership that's split 50/50 between two partners can end in a stalemate when it comes to making important decisions together. For this reason, many people prefer to split a partnership 45/45 giving the remaining 10% to a third party who can act as a "tie breaker" in the event that you and your main partner cannot come to an agreement.

I encourage you to take the time and thoroughly research each entity type. As mentioned before, this is only an overview. While researching, keep in mind the important factors that have been discussed above: liability, business expansion, taxes and paperwork, and personal relationships between partners. Only you can decide which risks you are comfortable taking. Taking the time to know how you want your business to run and what you want from your business will make it easier for you to know what to expect when entering the business world. Remember, "I didn't know" is not a valid answer to lawsuits and financial responsibility. Know your facts and act accordingly. You don't want to be stuck in a messy and frustrating situation while your business vision fizzles away!

Keywords:

Business Type: the structure or setup by which a business operates, both practically and legally. There are four common options: corporation, limited liability company, sole proprietorship, and partnership.

Corporation: a business type that uses shares in which liability is separate from employees and shareholders. Corporations are taxed separately from their owners. C corporations have unlimited shares and are worldwide. S corporations have limited shares that must stay in the United States.

Liability: legal responsibility.

Limited Liability Company (LLC): a business type with limited liability in which personal and business assets are separate. LLCs are taxed like individuals or sole proprietorships, not corporations.

Partnership: a business type in which multiple owners own, operate, and have full liability for the business.

Sole Proprietorship: a business type in which a single owner owns, operates, and has full liability for the business.

ACTION DIARY:

Date: _____

Which business structure is right for you?

What are the legal requirements for that business structure? (Hint: Contact your Secretary of State to discover the requirements of your chosen business.)

Will your business need special licensing? If so, what sort? Be sure to research all certifications and licensing needed for your business (e.g., goods, foods, services).

How will these startup costs affect your budget? Since startup costs are a part of your capital, be sure to include them in your financial plan.

Chapter 6
Cultivating the Home-Based Business

If what you have read so far sounds appealing to you and you would like to be your own boss and set your own hours, then a home-based business might be just the tool you need to cultivate your goals. Having a clear vision and understanding of what to expect is a good start, but there is more to the puzzle than dreaming and knowing; you also have to follow through and make your dream happen. This takes drive and action. So let's do the hard work and get your business off the ground!

Being noticed and making a good impact on your market are crucial parts of your business endeavor. If there is little demand for your product, doing this can be difficult. Likewise, if there are many similar products on the market, you need to demonstrate the superiority of your product in order to make yourself stand out.

Your Vision in Action

Now is the time to pick up where you left off after doing the research. Now is the time for you to define your vision and make it a reality. Now is the time to get your business out there.

How do you achieve this? Advertising!

Firstly, take a moment and write down some basic questions that consumers might have about your product or service. These questions will vary depending on the product or service you want to offer. The basic questions are:

- What are you selling?

- What do you want it to accomplish?

- What do you see your product doing for others?

You might also want to think about things such as: how does it work? Why is it different? What options are available? And of course, you'll need to bring in all your research about price points and costs, as well as thinking about things such as discounts for purchasing more than one item, or for paying for more than one hour of service. In short, think about the kind of questions you would have if you were the consumer. For example, perhaps your business fixes computers. If you saw a sign that just said "Computers Fixed," what questions would you have before you committed to contacting that company? Brainstorming as though you were the customer can be very useful.

Describe and sell your product like the world has never heard about it, even if it is a common product in the marketplace. Don't try and make consumers feel stupid, but do let them know what you're offering and what they can expect from it and from you. You don't have to know everything about the product, but knowing more than the average consumer goes a long way. The more the consumer feels you know, the more likely they are to inquire further, and the more likely they are to trust you as an expert in your field. Sell your product like you would want a product sold to you.

If you're having problems selling your product to yourself, go back to the notes you took when we first started talking about your vision. Look at the basic principle of your product or service and figure out where it fits into the business world. Knowing where you're going is the key to making sure you're marketing to the right audience. Take some time and outline your target audience. This will help you strategize a route and stick to it instead of stumbling along blindly.

And don't forget about all those keywords you found while thinking about your product. Utilizing some of these keywords will help customers find you, since these are the words they're likely to type into Google when searching for your product.

Example:

> You are going to start a house-cleaning business. Whom would this service benefit the most? Busy, working families. Trying to market such a service to housewives wouldn't get many customers, so you should focus on families that might not have the time to clean their homes the way they'd like to. What strategies would gain the attention of this targeted group? What keywords would people like this be interested in?

Know your niche, and market accordingly. One of the biggest mistakes you can make is not knowing in which direction you want your business to go; another is not knowing whom you want your product or service to benefit. Not knowing these things is essentially throwing your vision away.

You should also think about *where* you want to advertise your product, and that will depend a lot on who your target market is. Online advertising services such as Facebook advertising can help you target a market, though you will pay for their services. But even something as simple as flyers can work. You just have to make sure those flyers go to the right people. Sending out flyers for your new landscaping business to all the apartments in an apartment building isn't likely to net you much business, but sending out fewer flyers to all the large homes on a street will probably get you more clients.

Knowing the Pros and Cons of Home-Based Businesses and Making Them Work for You

Getting your business out there is one half of the battle. The other half is actually starting work. And if you choose to start your business from home, then there are a few factors you'll need to think about before actually setting up shop.

What do you envision when the term "home-based business" comes up? Do you see a person working in pajamas while watching daytime television? Or do you see a neat little desk in a corner where all of the work is done and, when the day is through, the desk is no longer used? Perhaps you see a workstation that is used part of the day, while the other part of the day is spent out of the house, taking care of necessary tasks. Every person has his or her own vision of a home-based business. But don't be fooled by wishful thinking. Starting and maintaining your own business is hard work. It takes time and effort to make a business run like a well-oiled machine. Be prepared to work hard, and don't think that just because you're working from home (possibly in your pajamas!) life is going to be relaxing and easy.

Do you have a clear vision of what your day is going to look like when you begin to operate your business? Most people have some idea of what they're in for, but not a complete understanding. Not considering some factors inherent in a home-based business can lead to a lack of motivation and commitment in the long run. Take a close look at yourself and your home situation and evaluate what could be a benefit or a hindrance to your business. While working from home can be a great thing, there are also downsides.

Do you have a family? A home-based business is a great way to have the extra time you want to spend with them. Making your own schedule allows great opportunities for getting involved with extracurricular activities and spending time with spouses, friends, and kids. However, having the kids around when you're trying to work can be distracting. Your children might not realize that you're working and need to devote your time and attention to your business. It's surprising how many people consider working from home not "real work," meaning that if you're not careful you can rapidly become the neighborhood babysitter or designated "receiver of packages," or that people will drop in for coffee or your spouse will expect you to run all the errands. It can be difficult to prioritize when working from home!

Do you enjoy doing what you want whenever you want? A home-based business is a great way to make your own schedule. However, making your own schedule can also hinder your business. If you're a procrastinator, you'll need to set yourself deadlines and come up with ways to make sure you do everything when it needs to be done. Lack of motivation can lead to a business failing. Make your work time work time. Set aside certain hours during your day that are specifically devoted to your business. On the flip side of this, it can also be difficult to switch off. Since your business is right there in your living room, it can be tough to "finish work" and give yourself some all-important chill-out time.

Do you have a working space devoted solely to your business? If not, then it is easy for your work life and your personal life to become tangled together. It's a good idea to have a space set aside for business use. This could be a small table in a corner or a whole room. Whatever the case, be sure to allocate space and tools specifically for your business. Doing so will alleviate the lack of a professional environment needed for your business and also prevent you from losing supplies.

There are many other helps and hindrances inherent in starting a home-based business. Think about your own situation and come up with which ones apply to you. If you know yourself well, then you can overcome your hindrances and run a successful home-based business. But it's best to outline some ground rules from the very beginning. Start with a suitable location, setting some work hours, and talking to friends and family about what you're doing and what you need.

Keyword:

> **Home-based Business**: any business in which the primary administrative work (and often the rest of the work as well) is done from the owner's home.

Have the Right Supplies

You want a great start to your business, right? Then you need to be prepared to start and succeed. This means having all you need at your fingertips. Have the supplies you know you will use, and make sure you have plenty of them! One of the biggest wastes of time is running out of a necessary supply and having to go get it.

"What are some of the necessary supplies my business needs?" is a list you should make. Know exactly what you're going to need in order to get started and maintain a good flow of productivity.

- Are you producing a product?

- What materials do you need in order to produce it?

- If you have a service, what do you need in order to perform this service with excellence?

Write down anything and everything you might need in order to ensure you're prepared to get started and run with limited roadblocks in your way.

As discussed above, getting your name out is one important component to your business. This means having necessary marketing materials such as flyers and business cards. There are many printing companies that will offer these services for a decent cost. If you're starting out small, then you will probably use mostly social media at first; but having other resources is also beneficial.

Office supplies are another big must-have. Make sure you have supplies for keeping your finances in order, sending correspondence, and storing records. Even if your business is a hands-on venture, you will need to keep records of your business transactions for tax time. Know where your time and money go. Don't think for a moment that you're going to remember every little detail you need to know in order to run a smooth business. Take the time and write it down. You will thank yourself later.

The other supplies you will need depend on the type of business you choose to operate. These might be a computer, an open space to work, or other materials that will make your business more efficient. Make a comprehensive list. When it comes to running your own business, it's better to have too much than not enough! And don't forget to keep all your receipts and note down what you spend on supplies, since come tax time you'll want to deduct these expenses.

By knowing what to expect and what you need, you are setting yourself up for success. You can never be over-prepared, but it is possible to be unorganized. There is a lot of competition in the business world, so knowing what you need and using it accordingly are key.

Now that you have what you need, the next step is: get out there and make your business known! Remember, a positive to your home-based business can turn into a distraction. Keep focused and motivated to fulfill your business vision.

ACTION DIARY:

Date: _____

Is a home-based business right for you? Why or why not?

What are some positive outcomes of starting your home-based business, and what are the negatives that will make you compromise?

What will be the cost of getting started? (Include costs such as buying a computer, software, and printer, and maintaining an Internet connection.)

Section Three
Monetize

Chapter 7
Your Product

There are all sorts of different products, and part of knowing the ins and outs of yours is identifying several key points. In this chapter, I'm going to give you information and suggestions on how to define your product and sell it to your intended audience. If you don't know your product, can't define or describe it, then you can't market it, and people won't buy it! So it's key that you know exactly what you're trying to sell (and whom you're trying to sell it to).

Different Types of Products

Millions of products are being marketed in the world, and new ones come out every day. These products have countless uses and purposes. The best way to find out more about your product is to see where it fits in with its competitors. Let's take a look at different types of products and services to see what they are all about. Fitting your product into a broad category will help you narrow down exactly what it is you're selling.

Tangible Products

The first genre of product is tangible products. This type of product lives up to its name. A tangible product is one that can be seen and touched. Examples of tangible products are cars, houses, toys, etc. If you own the physical copy of this book, you are holding a product that is a tangible product. If you're reading it on an e-reader, it is an intangible product, and your e-reader is a tangible product.

If you intend to sell an item, your product probably falls into this category. Tangible products are simpler to market because they are physical and easier to describe. A product that a consumer can pick up, examine, and touch tends to be easier to sell to the public, especially if you're opening a shop. But even online, a tangible product sold with lots of pictures gives the customer a better idea of exactly what they're receiving, making it an easier sell.

Intangible Products

Intangible products are less clear cut. An intangible product lacks a physical quality and is more of an idea. Examples of intangible products include things such as insurance policies, auto loans, and bank accounts. These are all products that are sold, but they are more of an idea or promise than a physical object.

Although the products listed above would be difficult to turn into a home-based business, there are other intangible products that are more accessible. Making online videos, selling digital media such as music and e-books, and writing a monetized blog are all examples of intangible products that make great home-based businesses. Knowledge and information are intangible products that are sold every day (and you might not even realize you're buying them!).

Services

The last category of products is services. A service is an act that your company provides on behalf of your customer. This ranges from lawn care to childcare. If you are doing something that someone else pays you to do, you are performing a service. Freelance designers, accountants, and all kinds of people provide services for a price. Your skills and knowledge can be very marketable as a service.

Services are as numerous as tangible products. A service can even create a tangible product.

Example:

> You are hired to make hats for orphaned children. You are performing a service for the person who hired you, and

you are creating a tangible product at the same time! The customer hired you for a service, even if it involves creating a tangible item.

Subcategories of Products

There are thousands of product subcategories, so I'm going to share one with you as an example. One subcategory of tangible, intangible, and service products is *information-based products.*

Information-based products are pretty much what you might think they are: information based. The purpose of these products is to teach someone about something. Nowadays, information-based products are very popular, particularly given the ease with which they can be created thanks to computers, the Internet, and easy-to-use software.

Tangible information-based products. One of the first information-based products you probably thought of is books. Many authors are in the market of selling information-based products. This genre is more than books, though! It can include magazines, flyers, brochures, language tapes, and the like.

Intangible information-based products. Information-based businesses may also be intangible, which is something you may not have considered.

Example:

> You want to design and promote businesses with your advertising company. This is an information-based endeavor. You are informing your audience about clients' businesses.

This genre of business can be as narrow or as broad as you want. However, if it's too broad, you may have trouble pinpointing your intended audience. This may mean your product is too simple and it's time to go back to the drawing board. Remember: you want your product to stand out, and standing out means being unique and interesting. So start thinking broad by choosing a wide category of products and knowing where you are in the market, but narrow down your choices later. There's a difference between "writing books" and "writing books to help people learn Japanese." And further, there's a difference between "writing books to help people learn Japanese" and "writing books to help English-speaking kindergarten children to learn Japanese." See how that last category has a specific market? You have a unique product and a defined target audience, both of which make for a good starting point for your business.

Service information-based products. Information may also be sold as a service. Private tutors for anything from mathematics to music to foreign languages are providing an information-based service.

Product Type Marketing

As you can see, type of products can be interwoven, and your business can cover more than one of these broad areas. It's important to fully know what you're marketing before you pursue advertising. Your advertising must reflect exactly what you're selling. Misrepresentative marketing can lead to lawsuits. Don't fall into that mistake! Even at best, marketing the wrong idea, product, or service will lead to confused consumers who won't buy from you because they don't know what you're selling!

Keywords:

> **Information-based product**: a type of product used for the purpose of distributing information. Information-based products may be intangible (e.g., commercials), tangible (e.g., books), or services (e.g., history lessons).

> **Intangible product**: a type of product produced by a business. Intangible products do not require action from the business from which they are purchased, and they do not have physical presence. Examples of intangible products are insurance policies and digital music.

> **Tangible product**: a type of product produced by a business. Tangible products do not require action from the business from which they are purchased, and they have a

physical presence. Examples of tangible products are chairs and automobiles.

Service: a type of product produced by a business. Services are actions taken by a business on behalf of a paying client. Examples of services are dog walkers and academic tutors. In some cases, services may produce tangible products (such as a photographer who then sells physical copies of the photos taken) or intangible products (such as a photographer who then sells digital copies of the photos taken).

Know What You're Selling

As stated above, it is extremely important to know what you're selling so you can market it correctly. This will require deep thought and observation. Take some time and get to know what you intend to sell before you jump in. Ask yourself questions and be able to describe your product inside and out before you market it. There are many questions to ask yourself here, some of which will depend on exactly what it is you're trying to do. However, below are some of the most common.

What Will Your Product Be Used For?

Take a long and scrutinizing look at your product and write down all of its uses. Even if you don't intend to market it for all of its potential uses, it's helpful to know them. You never know what you might want to expand!

Who Would Benefit From Your Product?

Again, take a long and scrutinizing look at your product. What type of person (or animal) would get the best use out of your product? If your product is aimed toward animal use, how can you market your product toward owners? Write down the groups of consumers you want to reach. Knowing your customer is one of the top ways of ensuring that your product will survive in the sales market. As we mentioned before, you need to market your product to your target audience to achieve maximum sales; don't waste your money advertising to people who won't or can't buy from you.

Example:

> You want to sell a device that will make cleaning up after a pet's outdoor bathroom activities easier. The top audience for your product will be pet owners. More specifically, pet owners whose animals go to the bathroom outdoors. The first animal that would come to mind would be a dog, right? Dog owners would most likely benefit from your product. You would be making a mistake if you tried to market your product to bird or reptile owners.

Know your audience. Know what type of person would most benefit from your product. One of the easiest ways to fail is going to the wrong consumer with your product.

Where Will Your Product Be Sold?

With the ever-growing market of Internet shopping, you really want to consider whether you'd benefit from selling in online stores, in physical stores, or in both. Regardless of how much you know about the Internet, you can benefit from using it.

Take a look around. Where do many people find what they want or need? A lot of people go to typical retail establishments, but many people also turn to the Internet to find products and services. Don't miss out on a great opportunity to sell your product or service just because you're intimidated by online retail! Research websites that offer seller shops, such as eBay and Etsy. See how setting up a store on one of these sites might benefit you. Setting up an online store is easier than you might think, and again, you'll find all the tutorials and knowledge you need for free online!

Knowing and Defining Your Product

Before you can sell something, you need to know what that something is. This is where your wonderful research skills come in handy. Take some time and look around at what you're interested in. There are two easy ways to go about this:

1. If you're computer savvy, take to the Internet and type keywords in a search engine to see what pops up. This is a great way to spark ideas.

2. If you prefer to look at physical products, go to stores that fascinate you and look at what they have on their shelves. Take some time and look at products in your interest area that actually *sell!* If it's going to gather dust on a shelf, then it might not be a profitable business venture.

Once you have determined what your product or service is going to be, take the time to observe and define what you're selling. Be able to describe everything from what it looks like (if it's tangible) to what it can be used for. Here are some questions to help you:

- How will your product benefit others?

- Is this a physical or intangible product or a service? What subcategories might it fit?

- What does the product look like?

- How is the product used?

- Why is your product better than your competitors' products?

The last thing a customer wants to hear are the words "I don't know." Be the expert in all areas of your business.

With the millions of products being bought and sold to a wide variety of people on a daily basis, knowing what you're selling and how it can benefit its audience is huge. Don't step blindly into the marketplace. Knowing your product or service is just as important as knowing the business world and what niche your business is going to fit into. Even though it seems boring and tedious when all you want to do is get started, it's a necessary component to being a successful entrepreneur.

ACTION DIARY:

Date: _____

What will your product be?

Who will benefit from your product?

Find other products like the one you plan to sell. List any area that may need improvement.

What is your niche?

How will you sell your product?

Chapter 8
Writing an E-book

In today's technological age, new terms are being created and thrown out there all the time. However, in reality, how familiar are we with these terms? One of the most used terms is "e-book." Have you ever wondered what exactly an e-book is and how the process of getting an e-book published happens? Have you considered writing your own e-book? As technology advances, you are more likely to see more forms of old-school technology, such as books, become computerized.

Creating an e-book that highlights your business can lead to even more success for your dream. Having an e-book available as a resource draws people who are interested in what you have to offer to them. Think about the times when you searched the Internet to find information or services. The businesses that offered more information drew you to them first because you didn't have to piece together a whole bunch of information from different resources. By providing extra information, you are offering your potential customers another service!

In this chapter, we are going to explore the e-book and what goes into one—from start to finish. You might be surprised how doable writing your own e-book for publication can be. If you have an inkling of writing your own book, whether fiction or nonfiction, you really must know the ins and outs of an e-book and how it could boost your business as a writer.

What is an E-book?

The first question we must answer is the most obvious of them all. What is an e-book? You can probably guess by the name itself that it is a book, but what kind? And what is the big deal about e-books? These are important questions. In order to write and explore e-books, you must first know what they are and how popular they are.

An e-book is a text that is designed to be read in an electronic format ("e-book" is short for "electronic book"). This can be done on a computer, e-reader, or any other device that supports e-books. E-books cover subjects as diverse as those you'd find at a local bookstore or library. You can even get children's picture books in electronic format! For many people, this type of book takes away the days of lugging around bulky, heavy books (although there are many who still prefer the old-fashioned feel of paper books that line the shelves of libraries).

E-books have become extremely popular in the past few years. There are numerous devices on the market today that support e-books, and many are specifically for reading books in electronic format. Sounds convenient, right? That's exactly why it's so popular. E-books are easily accessible and incredibly portable! However, not every book has been converted to an electronic format, so there might still be instances when you must step back in time and read a printed book.

Keyword:

> **E-book**: an electronic book that may be read on a computer, smart phone, e-reader, or other device.

What is So Special About an E-book?

Many people are driven by convenience. If it's easier, more accessible, and saves time, then people will want it. An e-book fits all of those categories. E-books are compact, easily obtainable, and can be quickly acquired. You can be at home on your computer and look at a book's description one minute and the next minute be reading the book. This eliminates the hassle of going to the library or the bookstore.

Not only are e-books convenient, but they are also environmentally friendly. Since they don't use paper to print the pages, e-books save trees. Many like that fact about them. As time goes on, increasing numbers of books are available in e-book format. Why not get into the market of e-books now?

Why Would I Want to Write and Sell an E-book?

So, you're wondering why you would want or need to write and sell an e-book. After all, your home-based business has absolutely nothing to do with writing or storytelling. The answer is that writing and selling your e-book can offer your customers valuable information about your business and your services. Not only can you make money with your business, but you can also profit from your e-book as well.

Don't get me wrong: I'm not suggesting that you write a book asking people to hire you or giving the sort of dimensions that belong in an owner's manual. Instead, I'm suggesting you write about the experience of your business and other things readers will find interesting and informative.

Example:

> Your business involves making toys for children. You write a book about your experiences in starting your business, the sorts of troubles you encountered, and your successes. You talk about toys in a way that the general public can understand and will find attractive, and about which toys children seem to like most. Although your book is, on a surface level, a story about your experiences, it's also a book-long advertisement for both your toys and your business.

Example:

> You're still a toymaker, but instead of writing about yourself, you write a children's story *about one of your toys*. Have you read *The Velveteen Rabbit* or *Winnie-the-Pooh*? Both of these books sold toys—and yours can, too!

E-books are a great marketing tool. By writing and publishing your own e-book, you have the opportunity to draw customers to your business. Someone might see your e-book during a web search, click on the link, and end up on your personal or business site! You not only have sold this person on the content of your book; you may have also found someone who is willing to invest in your business. It's a win-win situation!

How is an E-book Created?

Since e-books are in electronic format, there are differences in the way these books are formatted. There are numerous programs on the market that can help you get your e-book ready to be published electronically. As with other types of service, there are also companies and freelancers who will format your text for you.

As I mentioned before, there are many programs and services that can be used in order to format your text into an e-book. You can even do it yourself.

Let's look at the steps involved in creating an e-book from start to finish—including writing, editing, and publishing your e-book so that it will be readable on almost any device.

The first step is the most obvious. You must have good content to put into an e-book. That means you must write something that someone out there will want to read. Say, for example, you're in the business of landscaping and you decide that you want to publish a guide on unique landscaping. First of all, you want this book to stand out from the rest of the many books in the same genre. Take some time to outline and carefully write your content. Make sure it's complete, logical, and, most importantly, professionally edited. From there, you are ready to continue the process of making your book into an electronic success!

The next big step is to figure out the ideal layout for your book. Are you planning on including pictures? Diagrams? Charts? It is extremely important that you know exactly how you want your finished project to look on an e-reader. From there, you are able to find which programs or services can make that happen for you. If you have software that will do the trick, then you're already set! Make sure you're following all of the steps necessary in order to make your book publishable.

Another area you must consider is a book cover. Yes, even e-books must have captivating covers to grab readers' attention. Take time and effort when considering your e-book's cover. You want it to portray the content of the e-book, and you don't want it to mislead the person who reads it. That's a common frustration with books. You think you're reading one thing, but then it's totally different.

Along with the book cover will be your title. Again, you want to make sure your title accurately portrays what your book is really about.

If you don't want to create your own cover, there are plenty of companies and freelancers available who specialize in cover design. Do a little research. You can buy premade covers (on which the designer will put your name and title) or commission a cover designer (be sure to look at the designer's other covers first to make sure you want something similar).

A couple of things to keep in mind:

1. If you want to get an e-book out there and have a great idea but don't have the time or skill to write it yourself, you can hire a ghostwriter to do it for you.

2. It is essential that you hire an editor. It's tempting to try to edit your own work, but this is always a mistake. If your book isn't properly edited, your readers will notice . . . and they will leave negative reviews, dramatically lessening your sales.

3. There are plenty of companies and freelancers out there who can help you with any or all stages of publishing your book, from writing to editing to interior formatting to cover design. Using a single company to help you along every step of the process can save time and lower stress.

Different Writing Techniques

After learning what an e-book is and how it can help your business, it is now time to write one! Most authors claim that the hardest part of producing a good quality e-book to the market is not the publishing process but the writing part. Remember writer's block? It is struggling to put ideas swarming in your brain to words. And for every writer who thinks the writing process is the hardest, there's one writer who thinks the marketing is hard. We'll cover both tips here. So if you struggle with one and not the other, feel free to gloss over the parts you have no problem with. You won't hurt my feelings. And most first-time authors have issues of some kind with the publishing process, so we'll go over that too.

So, you ask, what does it take to write an e-book? Here are some writing techniques to help with the writing struggle after deciding on the niche you want to write about.

1. *Create an Outline of the Topic*

    Before you actually start writing your e-book, create a good outline for you to follow; otherwise, you'll be lost in the sea of ideas. When you have an outline composed of chapters, break it down to sub-chapters to easily convey points and important information, as well as make it easy for your readers' eyes. Think and visualize your e-book as far as what's going into the beginning, the middle, and the end to make creating sub-chapters a breeze.

2. *Starting Small but Consistently*

    Many authors make it a point to write at least one page of their e-book daily. If time is an issue, a 300-word page is enough to add to your e-book. Numerous successful authors follow this mantra until they're ready to do more every single day. Some write a single page when they don't feel like it, and push to several pages when their creative juices are flowing. We're just humans; we get tired too, but we also get an adrenaline rush when we're presented with inspirations. So don't worry if you have one-page days, as it is just the norm!

3. *Find a Unique Place to Write*

It doesn't have to be fancy. It just needs to be a different place from where you're doing other activities. It is best not to write your e-book in a bedroom; you'll be distracted to go take a nap every time you feel sluggish. Set a place where your inspirations are visible in writing this e-book. For example, if your topic is about food, decorate that place with food images or put your cookbooks, recipe books, and other materials you're going to use in that room. The point is that, when you enter the room, it will prompt you to write more, helping the creative juices to flow.

4. *Set a Time for Writing Daily*

Apart from having a unique place to write, it is also essential to set a time for you to work on your e-book every single day. If you're a mom with small kids that need to be cared for, it is best to write when they're already asleep so no one can distract you. Or if you are also an entrepreneur who is busy during the middle of the day, you can set every early morning and late evening to be your writing time.

5. *Give a Deadline for Yourself*

Without a deadline, you'll procrastinate. This is the sad truth! So be accountable and set a deadline for yourself. A good weekly deadline of number of words or progress percentage will help you reach your goal. Have something to aim for every week and find someone who will hold you accountable for it. My editor would like for me to put in here: don't use an editor as your accountability. Apparently, writers will book editors for a certain date and can't keep their appointment, causing their rather hefty down payments to be lost. Or worse yet, spending a fortune on last-minute ghostwriting.

6. *Don't be Afraid to Fail and Write Another*

All authors are embarrassed of their first books, and many get lots of rejections before their books are published. The journey to get your first e-book out there will be hard and messy for sure, but embrace failure and be positive about it. Your high standards of perfection will not sustain you. Learn the lessons of creating your first e-book and practice. This is the only way for you to get good at it. So make your work available to everyone, fail early, and then try again.

Once you have this all together, you're ready for the next step: publication!

Keywords:

Editing: a service in which the customer pays a professional editor to improve a book. There are different types of editor, so make sure you do some research before hiring one.

Ghostwriting: a service in which the customer pays a professional writer to write a specific book. Traditionally, ghostwriters are not credited for their work.

Publishing and Marketing

Perhaps you don't have problems with the writing bit, but self-publishing gives you a headache.

Self-Publishing Your E-book

It is very challenging to create an e-book, especially for first-timers who are not familiar with the different processes. However, the e-book industry is rapidly evolving and many publishing companies are introducing new platforms and special features that make the creation of an e-book a lot faster and easier.

Many authors are becoming frustrated with the difficulties associated with the traditional publishing process. This is probably one of the reasons why new writers and authors today are opting to self-publish their works using platforms such as Amazon KDP and NOOK Press.

Where to Self-Publish Your E-book?

This is the big question for everyone. What is so great about these self-publishing platforms is that they offer so much convenience for the authors. If you know how to use MS Word and navigate the web through Google, then you can self-publish your e-book. Most of the platforms available today do not require you to have any technical knowledge in programming. If the thought of formatting your book yourself makes you break out in hives, you can hire someone to format it for you. Prices start as low as $25.

The most popular platforms you can try for e-book self-publishing include:

- Amazon KDP

- Barnes & Noble NOOK Press

- Kobo Writing Life

- iBooks Author

- Smashwords

Some Good Tips When Self-Publishing Your E-book

Start with an eye-catching cover. – There is a saying that you should not judge a book by its cover. However, when it comes to actual books and e-books, your cover image has to grab the attention of the readers. It has to be eye-catching or professional-looking, which could make a big difference. Also, you have to think about certain images that would also look good as thumbnail images when sold online. If you don't know how to create a good cover, you can hire a graphics designer who is experienced in making e-book covers. Good places to check out are Upwork, TheGhostwritingAgency.com, Guru, or Fiverr. You can find a variety of freelancers to help you with pretty much anything on your book, whether editing, proofreading, formatting, or cover design, and even writing, on such freelance sites.

You should set the price for your e-book. – It's your e-book, and you should be the only one who can set the price that you want for it. If you encounter a self-publishing outfit that doesn't allow you to set the price of your e-book, you should get out immediately.

Don't overprice your e-book. – We understand you want to make a profit out of your e-book. However, overpricing or placing an expensive price on your e-book creation may have a negative impact on your sales. Some experts say that e-books with a price tag from $1 to $3 outsell others that have a much higher price range. There are a variety of support groups for self-publishing authors on Facebook, such as Pat's First Kindle Book, which can help you gauge whether you've set prices right.

If you need help formatting or with cover design, there are tons of options on the Internet. Checking out freelance sites like Upwork will give you a plethora of designers and formatters to choose from. It will cost you a few pennies, but when you're attempting the book process for the first time, the extra help may be advantageous for you.

Amazon KDP

Amazon Kindle Direct Publishing is Amazon's e-book publishing platform. Amazon has been dominating the book market for years, and this is a very good reason why so many authors prefer to self-publish their e-book on this popular platform.

When it comes to the royalty rate for authors, Amazon offers 70 percent. Amazon also offers incentives for authors who will sell their e-book exclusively with Amazon. They call it the KDP Select, which makes your e-book eligible to be included in the Kindle Owner's Lending Library, where you can earn a share of the fund based on how frequently the book is borrowed. You are also provided new promotional tools to help market your e-book.

NOOK Press by Barnes & Noble

Barnes & Noble has its own self-publishing platform, which is called the NOOK Press. By using the NOOK Press website, you can submit your e-book on the Barnes & Noble website. You can use your Barnes & Noble account to log in to your NOOK Press account. You can also create a brand new account, but keep in mind that each email address can only be used once.

Kobo Writing Life

Kobo or KWL is another popular self-publishing platform where it only takes a few steps to publish your work. When you use KWL, your e-book can be purchased in the Kobo store. If your e-book is priced from $1.99 to $12.99, Kobo pays you 70% royalty. If your e-book is priced outside of this range, you receive a 45% royalty.

iBooks Author

When it comes to graphic-rich e-books and multi-touch interactive e-books, the iBooks Author is a very good choice. With this platform, your e-book will be confined to the Apple iBookstore. However, you have to keep in mind that Apple, creator of the iPad, iPhone, and iPod, is still a very strong brand with millions of users all over the world. The iBooks Author is ideal for photography, children's books, cookbooks, and other e-books with lots of images and graphics. It is free to download for Mac users with a good selection of templates and multitouch widgets. It offers a royalty rate of 70% throughout.

Smashwords

If you think that you want to go as wide as possible in distribution, Smashwords is the place to go. Smashwords will upload your book to all platforms except Amazon. You can easily do this in one click. You'll still get all the royalty rates as you would if you uploaded them yourself. The only downside to Smashwords is that their formatting requirements are a little grueling, but instead of fixing things to several different formats, you'll only have to do one.

In conclusion: consider writing an e-book for your business and using it as a marketing resource. The advantages to helping your business grow and expand are numerous. E-books are easy to publish and relatively inexpensive to use as a promotional tool—but poorly written or unedited e-books can do more harm than good, so you need to make sure you're committed to producing a quality product before continuing.

Allow today's technology to help you and your business grow and succeed. Offer your clientele the information and the resources that will make your business shine!

ACTION DIARY:

Date: _____

Do you think you have information that could help others?

Take the time to write down talking points and other valuable information for your e-book.

Buy a popular e-book from your niche category. Read it and figure out at least five ways the e-book could be better.

Start writing your e-book by piecing together the information you've collected. No need to worry about making the first draft perfect; you will have it edited later. The first thing is to get it down on paper!

Chapter 9
Affiliate Marketing

If, after reading the bulk of this book, you realize a) yes, you want to start your own business, and b) yes, you want the freedom of being your own boss . . . you're on your way to success. But what if you are good at selling things but don't know *what* to sell? In fact, what if you'd like to own your own business but sell other people's products?

Don't worry—there's a way to do this. If that doesn't sound like you, keep reading anyway—you might want to hire an affiliate marketer one day.

There are many people out there who start their own business but lack the time or imagination and creativity to market their products. As you know, in order for your product or service to sell, you have to advertise it and spread the word about it. There are plenty of business owners and companies out there willing to hire the services of others in order to achieve this goal.

What is Affiliate Marketing?

Just what or who performs this task of advertising? Some companies have their own marketing departments, but many don't have the means to devote an entire department to promotion. The owners of those companies may decide to take up affiliate marketing. Affiliate marketing is the process of hiring individuals or businesses to sell a business's product or service for it. The person who performs this task works on commission.

Essentially, working in affiliate marketing means making a commission off of selling someone else's product. The more you sell, the more you earn. The best news is: if the company is a total dud, you can always do affiliate marketing for other companies. Affiliate marketing gives you the freedom to choose what you want to do and when you want to do it. You can do as much or as little as you would like.

Sounds easy, right? There's a caveat: only people who have a knack for sales do extremely well with this type of work. You don't get paid for affiliate marketing until the business you work for reaps the fruit of your labors, which means your success as an affiliate marketer depends upon your ability to sell products and services. If you don't have the charisma to do such things, affiliate marketing may not be for you. However, if you can see yourself selling others' products, affiliate marketing is a great way to make money!

Keyword:

> **Affiliate Marketing**: a process by which an individual or business earns a commission by promoting the products of other businesses.

Pros and Cons of Affiliate Marketing

As with every business, there are pros and cons to affiliate marketing. It's best to know what these are before getting started so that there are no surprises waiting for you.

The Pros

Great Way to Earn Extra Money

Affiliate marketing offers you the opportunity to earn as much or as little as you are willing to work for. If you already have a day job and want to test the waters of affiliate marketing, doing so is a simple process. The way affiliate marketing works is that you get paid for your results. Depending upon the company you're marketing for, you may get paid for your personal performance. If you're a great salesperson, someone who can sell a bottle of sand in the desert, then you can do well in affiliate marketing no matter how much time you put into it.

With the flexibility of doing as much or as little as you want, you have the potential to earn as much or as little as you want.

Choose Your Own Hours

Want to work when you want to work? Affiliate marketing is a great way to make this a reality. If you want to keep your day job and just do affiliate marketing a few evenings a week, then you can. You get paid for your performance. If you do little, then your earning potential is less. If you work full time, your earning potential is greater. This allows for unlimited flexibility.

Choose What You Promote

With affiliate marketing, you have the opportunity to work for the companies you want to work for. If you have issues with promoting certain types of products, don't worry: you don't have to promote them. You can choose the type of company and product that works best for you.

The Cons

Those were a few of the pros of affiliate marketing. Once you get established and start making a decent income, then you can work on numerous marketing opportunities. If you decide that affiliate marketing's not for you, you easily can explore other avenues.

As with everything, affiliate marketing has its downsides. It's up to you to decide whether the pros outweigh the cons. I'm going to talk about a few of the cons of affiliate marketing and what you should look for—and look out for.

Pay is Based on Performance

Pay is based not only upon your personal performance, but also upon the performance of the product you're marketing. If the product is junk and there's no way you can sell it, you won't make any money from it no matter how much work you put in.

When choosing companies and products to do affiliate marketing with, make sure that you personally think the company is worthy and has a sellable product. It's your income on the line if the product doesn't work out. You don't want to work for nothing, do you?

Technology is Taking Its Place

Affiliate marketing is becoming a less useful form of promoting a business because of the wonderful world of technology and the Internet. It's gotten to the point where many companies can easily advertise their products on sites using search engines without the help of a third party, and therefore may not feel the need to pursue individuals for marketing. Don't lose hope, though. Affiliate marketing is still a large portion of advertising, which makes it a great opportunity for those willing to put in the work.

Unethical Practices

Another important thing for you to keep an eye on is how a company tracks its performance. There have been companies that have forced consumers to click on their ads, have installed adware on unwary users' computers, and have used other unethical methods to make consumers take notice of products or services. If you're anything like me, you hate it when popup ads force you to acknowledge them. It makes me not want the advertised product. Before you start working, make sure that you're not doing anything you wouldn't want done to you!

There are other positives and negatives to affiliate marketing. Some of these you will need to experience for yourself. If you're determined and willing to take on the pros and the cons of this type of marketing, then it's time to learn how to get started making money!

Getting Started With Affiliate Marketing

Affiliate marketing is often regarded as passive income because you have the potential to steadily earn money while you're just staying at home. The best thing about affiliate marketing is that anyone with the right attitude can do this and there are only a few requirements needed for entry. In order to get started as an affiliate marketer, there are several steps you have to follow. If you are the type of person who is determined, focused, and willing to put some time and effort into this project, then you have a good chance of succeeding.

Now that you have a better mindset about affiliate marketing, let's get started!

Find Your Affiliate Program

The first step is to do more in-depth research about affiliate programs that are most suitable for your niche, which we already did our dreaming about, right? Choosing the right program is very important because this is going to be your source of income. When choosing your affiliate program, you have to remember these important key points:

- The affiliate program should generate sufficient return on investment. Look for commission rates they are offering for the products.

- The products or services to be promoted should be of good quality.

- The affiliate program should have a reliable customer support that is always available.

Build Your Website

Building a website is not as complicated as you may think. It is actually much easier now to build a website that is relevant to your niche. One of the most common and best sites to help you start your website is WordPress.com. If you are a beginner, WordPress is the most recommended tool because it won't require any coding skills or technical knowledge during setup. An even easier option is to try a more visual website builder like Weebly.

Buying a domain and hosting is your first step when building a website. The domain is going to be the address of your website, and the hosting is the actual place where your website can be found. The domain and hosting are very affordable, and you can easily find the best service when you do your own research. The next step is creating your website and placing good contents relevant to your niche. We'll cover this topic more in depth in the next chapter.

Produce Great Content on Your Website

The best way to get a bigger audience and drive traffic to your website is to create interesting and exciting content. Unleash your inner creativity and find ways to produce more attractions that will keep your audience hooked and interested. Your goal is make excellent content to build a good image and establish your site as an authority on your particular niche.

Content is King

This is especially true when establishing your website as a major player in your niche. You can create product reviews that are very helpful for your audience. If your reviews are done well, it can be a great source of affiliate income.

You can also create blog posts that talk about everyday issues and topics everyone can relate to. You can come up with questions or issues that are relevant to your target audience. It would be helpful to include SEO keywords in your blog content.

Join an Affiliate Program

Finally, it's time to join an affiliate program and promote affiliate offers. Now that you've established yourself in your niche with a solid website and a respectable number of audiences, it's time to put your affiliate marketing skills into high gear. Many people fail with affiliate marketing because most of them skip the process of creating good content and building an audience and dive straight into the affiliate program. As we've mentioned earlier, you will have to do important tasks that will benefit your affiliate marketing.

Key Points to Remember When Joining an Affiliate Program:

A good affiliate program never asks for any upfront fee. If it asks for your credit card, you should be careful because it might be a scam. In most cases, they will ask for your website or URL and your bank account or PayPal account to facilitate payment of your commissions and earnings.

Getting started with affiliate marketing is all about consistency and your relentless pursuit of creativity, promotion, and innovation.

Affiliate Marketing Network Sites

You already have a good idea about affiliate marketing and how to get started. Now you need to know which affiliate marketing networks are most suitable for you. Some of the best affiliate programs recommended by most marketers include:

- Clickbank

- CJ Affiliate

- Amazon Associates

- Rakuten Linkshare

- Adwords from Google

Usually, these networks don't ask for any fee when you are joining their affiliate programs, with the exception of Google, but they're Google and get better results. The services being offered often include a central database of their available affiliate programs, analytics, reporting tools, and efficient payment processing. The programs may be arranged by category or popularity, which makes it more convenient for the affiliate marketers.

Payout Models

Each affiliate program has its own type of payout model. These models usually consist of: Cost Per Action (CPA), Cost Per Click (CPC), Cost Per Lead (CPL), and Cost Per Sale (CPS).

Cost Per Action (CPA) – You get paid for a specific action. These actions can be in the form of downloads, registers, sig- ups, submissions, or surveys.

Cost Per Click (CPC) – This simply pays you for every click done, whether it resulted in a sale or not.

Cost Per Sale (CPS) – You get a commission for a lead that resulted in an actual sale.

Cost Per Lead (CPL) – This is a type of payout that gives a commission for a successful lead. This is usually in the form of a sign-up with the customer's email address or credit card verification.

Choose a Trustworthy Vendor

Choosing a vendor should not always be based upon the commission rate being offered. You have to investigate further and see if the vendor's page is legitimate and trustworthy. Remember, if you advertise a product that is low quality, then your credibility as an affiliate marketer suffers and you won't generate any sales. So even if you see an 85% commission rate but the vendor is not trustworthy, then you should walk away and look for other vendors offering a much better product. ClickBank has over 6 million products, but not all of them are good quality, so you have to be smart in choosing the products you want to promote.

Generate Affiliate Link

When you are done choosing the products you want to promote, your next step is to generate your affiliate link. You have to use ClickBank's tracking ID feature so you can accurately track where your sales are coming from. Once you have set up your affiliate link and the tracking ID, you are now officially a ClickBank affiliate marketer. All you have to do now is to drive traffic into your website or blog so that your affiliate link can have its much-needed exposure.

Key Strategies:

Always create good content for your website to generate traffic. More traffic to your website means you have greater potential to earn with ClickBank. You can write a good article to attract readers and then show them your ClickBank affiliate offer located within the article. Another good strategy is to develop a newsletter for your website that promotes your ClickBank offers.

Summary

There is no rule that says you can only have an account with one affiliate marketing network. You can choose to have one in ClickBank and another in Amazon Associates; it is all up to you. If you don't want to make it too complicated, you can just work with one affiliate marketing network. It is also difficult to say which service provider is most suitable for you. The best way to find out is to get out there and experience it for yourself. Remember to constantly analyze your web traffic and find out the interests of your audience. With the right affiliate program, there is a big possibility that you can start earning money in no time at all.

ACTION PLAN

Date: _____

Write down the pros and cons of affiliate marketing.

Create a plan on starting with affiliate marketing.

What affiliate marketing network are you going to use? Are you going to use one or a combination of both? Why?

Finalize your plan for an affiliate marketing campaign.

Chapter 10
Exposing Your Business on the Internet

Now that you have already managed to get your ideas together and start something big, like your own business, you have to start growing it. You already know that being your own boss can have a lot of benefits, but did you ask yourself how to maintain those benefits and keep them flowing? One way to do this is to show what you have to offer online, through websites, blogs, and landing/sales pages.

Your website plays a very important part in your business. Through it, you attack the online environment. You have to keep in mind that you can't grow your website without doing SEO (search engine optimization). This is the process through which you manage to get traffic on your website with the help of search engines. If you do it right and put in a bit of hard work, you will see that if you search for your products or services, they will appear on the first page of Google, Bing, or Yahoo search results.

If you use a website to promote your business, you make a great choice because people nowadays use the Internet for anything, even for ordering food from the grocery store. It is the best way to make your products or services known quickly and easier than handing out brochures on the street or in mailboxes.

Your website offers more information about your type of business, and you as a company, than any other way you can choose to make yourself known. You can design a really complex website with images and descriptions of products and with any other information you want, or you can create a simple site where you put your contact information and some text describing who you are.

What Do These Pages Do?

Web, landing, and sales pages help you to boost your business and gain product exposure. By having one or all of these pages, you make your website available to anyone with a search engine. (See Chapter 4 to learn about keyword research.) This leads to potential clients and revenue! Websites are an extremely useful means of advertising, although they do not replace traditional means.

Having a website is also cost effective. By putting yourself out there on the Internet, you are opening yourself up to a greater customer base at a small cost. Take some time with a search engine and look at topics and items that interest you. Make a list of which landing pages, websites, and sales pages catch your eye, and then study them to discover why you like them best.

How are "Website," "Web Page," "Landing Page," "Blog," and "Sales Page" Different?

Website

Each website is written in its own language, HTML, and is designed to achieve a desired effect or impression. There is a lot of fine detail that goes into making an eye-catching website, and it takes an expert to make a good one.

Not computer savvy? Don't worry! There are services and programs out there that will help you to build a personal website. You can find such programs at a physical or Internet-based computer retailer or website design specialist. You can even download directions, if you want to try to build your website yourself.

Remember: a good website engages its visitors. It helps consumers experience your product or service before purchasing it. Take a look at popular websites that sell top products. Do you feel like you know their products before you purchase them? Do you feel you could use their product based upon the descriptions and graphics the web page offers? Yes? Excellent! Try to make your product website just as great.

Web Page

Each individual screen (or "page") on a website is called a web page.

Landing Page

A landing page is also part of a website, and it is a type of web page. Think of it as the cover of a book. You get a sense of what the book is like based on its cover—and, no matter what the popular wisdom, you judge the book by the cover. Landing pages do the same thing: they are covers for websites or advertisements for products or services.

Example:

> A person is doing a web search on the product you sell. When this person goes into the search engine and types in the keywords, a search results page is filled with websites that sell similar products. These websites offer short descriptions of what they are about, highlighting the keywords the user searched for. If a person clicks on a website, the first thing he or she will see is the landing page. This page gives the user an idea of what the website includes. Many people decide whether to delve further into the website based on the landing page.

What draws you to a product or service? When you go on the Internet to search for what you're looking for, which landing pages catch your attention? Try and use some of their elements when designing your own page. A good landing page leads to more sales and better business!

Sales Page

A sales page is another important component to making a great website. This is the page where you "close the deal." This is the page that sells your product. You want to make sure this page is engaging, interesting, and effective. On your sales page, you're not trying to lead or lure someone to your site; you're taking the people already on the site and selling something to them.

What do you typically see on a sales page? Take a look at a few that you like to visit and buy products from. The first thing you typically see is the product. You want to have a good picture of what you're selling so that those viewing it want to have it. Point out all of its good features. If it already has ratings, then you might want to display those if they're positive.

The next thing you will typically see is the price of the product. Let's be honest: it's annoying to look at a product and not be able to find its price. Are they hiding the fact that it's overpriced? Or did they just forget that major detail? Either way, make sure that your prices are listed on your page. Let the consumer know what you're charging. If it's too expensive, potential customers will move on anyway. Don't waste their time and annoy them by leaving this key detail out.

Most importantly, make sure you have a "Buy Now" or "Add to Cart" button, and make sure it's large and colorful!

Blogs

Here comes the other type of promotion you can choose, the blog. It is a type of website used for forums, online diaries, editorial sections of newspapers for expressing ideas, or other areas like politics, parenting, video games, and the like. You can choose to use a blog if you provide services or products that don't need a complex description. A blog is easier to edit and manage manually. You don't need a specialized company to provide you with a blog, like in the case of a website. You can make your own blog just the way you like it and promote your business in your own way.

A blog can be the first step you take in exposing your ideas and goals online. You can offer less information at first so that your clients will come and look for you out of curiosity. Or you can make both a website and a blog attached to it, a forum perhaps for testimonials and impressions. You should be clever when you choose the way to promote yourself online, because once you gain a good image, you can easily ruin it.

How Do I Start My Own Page?

Are you ready to go on the Internet with your business? Well, if you are, you're in the right place!

The first thing you need to consider is what you want your website to achieve. Do you want to sell your product? Or are you trying to be informational with the hope of selling yourself? When starting your website, you need to know your aim.

On social media, which will be covered in the next chapter, you will see a lot of people promoting themselves and their products on pages on a social network. Having your own website is similar. You want to make sure you are presenting not only yourself but also your product or service.

The key to getting the right style of website is knowing what you're aiming for. If you are focused on advertising, a simple informational web page might help. If you want to lead someone into your website with the intent of "closing the sale," then you want to consider a great landing page. If you're completely straightforward, then go for the gold with a sales page!

As mentioned before, there are different methods of creating your website. Which direction you go depends on you and your comfort level with technology. The first option is to create your own website. This requires a great knowledge of HTML formatting and the workings of the Internet.

The next option is to purchase software that will help you create your page. There are many software options, so know what you're aiming for before investing. This is great for those who know something about technology but aren't computer geniuses.

The last option is hiring a computer genius to create a website for you. This option can be costly because computer geniuses know their worth. If you went this route, the person you hired would take your vision and create a website that would draw people to you. Those who lack technological savvy tend to take this route.

Whatever option you choose for making your website, make it yours. Have a set idea of what you want on your website, what you want the pages to look like, and what you would like to see when you view it. Getting excited for your own website? What will you put on yours?

Keywords:

> **Landing Page**: a type of web page. This is the home page of any website. It is designed to be the first page viewers come across when accessing a website and functions much like a book cover by giving viewers a basic overview of what to expect in the rest of the website. Landing pages traditionally also give users easy access to other web pages within a website. The only page that might come before a landing page is a splash page.

> **Sales Page**: a type of web page that actively sells a product. It typically includes a product's name, description, image, and price, and a "Buy Now" or "Add to Cart" button that allows visitors to purchase the advertised product.

> **Splash Page**: a specific type of pre-landing page that contains only a graphic, such as a product image or business logo, on which users must click to access the landing page. In some cases, splash pages are used to allow visitors to pick their preferred language.

> **Web Page**: a web document suitable for the Internet. In simpler terms, it is any individual screen viewable on a website.

> **Website**: a set of associated web pages functioning under the same domain name. Websites are extremely useful tools for marketing to an Internet-savvy customer base.

Different Website Platforms for Your Business

Most of the time, finding the most suitable website platform for your business will depend on your budget and design specifications. There is no perfect website platform, and each of them offers unique features and specialties that can provide certain advantages for your business. There are so many e-commerce platforms available today, so it is recommended that you do your research before you choose one. There are content management systems (CMS), which are much more flexible and easier to use but lack some features that are available in other CMS. Here are some of the most common and popular website platforms you can look into when you are ready to create your business website.

WordPress

WordPress is the most popular and CMS available today. Millions of people are using it to create good-looking and highly functional e-commerce websites. Small- to medium-sized websites are most suitable for WordPress, and it is also preferred by many small e-commerce stores. If you are eyeing WordPress as your ideal platform, you may want to look at the reasons why it is the leading CMS in the market today.

It's absolutely free to use and perfect for startup business and small businesses that don't have a big budget for their website. Many of its plug-ins and themes are also provided for free and readily available for users.

You don't need to be a technical wizard to learn how to install WordPress. There are web hosting companies that offer an automated WordPress install, which only takes a couple of minutes. Getting a new website is much faster with the WordPress easy and fast installation process.

Adding posts, pages, products, media, and new content is made easier in WordPress. If you are a beginner, you can easily access helpful guides that will immediately solve your problems. Operating and making changes in WordPress can be done even without any knowledge of HTML coding.

Since WordPress is so popular, it has many helpful contributors in its support forum who can answer your questions and solve your website issues. You can access the support forum anytime for free.

Wix

Wix is another very popular website builder that is preferred by many because of its great features. It is considered a drag-and-drop website builder because you can literally drag and drop any content you want into your website. This means there is no technical coding required when customizing or making changes to your website.

Just like WordPress, it is also free and is preferred by many beginners and small-business owners. Wix offers a number of pre-designed templates that you can easily modify to make your site more customized. There are over 500 professional-looking templates you can choose from with graphics and themes that cover a broad range of industries.

Wix wants its users to be updated with the latest tools and features for website design. The new features can help improve your website and keep up with your competitors in the industry. The designs are also updated and provide so many options for your website. You can create a website with different background sections, or you can place background videos that look professional and dynamic.

Weebly

Weebly is another drag-and-drop website builder that is very easy to use. Once you access its user interface, you will be surprised by how minimal and simple it is, which makes website building a much easier process. You can easily learn its features, and the website building is very intuitive. So if you are not so tech savvy with website building, Weebly may be a great choice.

If you want to create a more customized design, Weebly allows you access to the design codes. You may need some basic knowledge in coding, but this added feature can really make a difference when it comes to creating professional-looking designs.

Weebly continues to update and provide better design templates for its users. In terms of technical support, it provides email and phone support that is always available. You may not even need the support team because Weebly is really easy to use.

What Should Be on My Page?

The first thing a visitor typically sees, either on a landing page or a sales page, is one or more color images of the product or products being sold. More advanced websites scroll between multiple attractive images that encourage the visitor to click on the product.

1. **A Simple Web Address that Makes Sense**

   Like a true friend, avoid making things complicated. Your domain name also serves as your brand. It should be easy for someone to remember and type. Using the .com domain is a prudent choice. Most net users are accustomed to typing that extension whenever they enter a web address.

   You can also opt to use a .org domain, but it is recommended to also have a .com version in case the user inadvertently types the .com extension. It is also wise to avoid using dashes and numbers in your web address.

2. **Site Map that is Easy to Navigate**

   A site map and links to the most important pages are important for directing your site visitors to the information that they want. Your website navigation must be clearly laid out. It is recommended to use dropdowns in the menu to give visitors an idea of what can be found under each heading.

3. **Contact Information that is Easy to Find**

   Make sure that your contact number is easy to find. It is recommended to put it on the upper left or right corner of your home page. It is also a good practice to include your contact information on every page.

4. Customer Testimonials

Sincere words from your customers help create more tangible products and services to online customers. The testimonials can help foster trust between "friends," and that helps a lot if you are new.

5. Call to Action

Don't forget to directly tell your online visitors what you want them to do. For instance, you may want them to sign up for your free membership, ask for a free quote, or add products to their virtual shopping cart and others. You need to use special buttons that highlight the action you want your online visitors to take.

6. Landing Page

Landing pages contribute a lot to lead generation, yet most businesses don't use them enough and some don't use them at all. Your landing page must have a killer headline that commands attention. You need a follow-up persuasive sub-headline to keep your readers even more interested. A picture paints a thousand words—make sure to use the right images that convey the things you want your readers to know in a glance and make them want to know more about the things you offer. Your explanation must be precise, concise, and mustn't create any misunderstanding. Make everything attractive and promising in the eye of your reader.

7. Site is Secure Logo

You need to put your customers at ease by letting them know it is perfectly safe to conduct business with you. It is important to let them know their personal data is safe with you by securing an SSL certificate for your site.

Example:

Having this logo in your site is proof that it is secure.

Keywords:

Strategic locations: It is important to place the important pieces of information on the places where your visitors can easily take notice of them. Don't make your visitors or potential clients go through all the pages just because you failed to provide proper site navigation.

Balanced and well designed: Make your blog page charming and its content interesting to make your visitors want to come back for more.

Attention grabber: Make sure your landing page has a killer headline and images that can easily grab attention.

Honest: Remember that your visitors want fresh, original, honest, and reliable information.

Summary:

There are other elements on a website that you might choose to include, but the three above are the absolutely necessary ones. Make your pages engaging and eye catching (but not eye scorching or you might drive away business). Use colors and themes that are pleasing to look at and are a good match for your product and its personality!

A website with a landing page, a sales page, and other web pages can be crucial to your business. Know what sells and try to make your website duplicate those features. You're not going to be able to please everyone, but you need to be up front and honest about what you're selling, what it's good for, and how much it costs. Beyond that, there are many different routes to take to a successful website. Just make sure that your page reflects your vision before you allow it to be published!

Making a website is a big step in saying that you have a business and that you're ready to sell. Congratulations on making it to this point!

Keywords:

> **Backlink**: a link from another website connecting a visitor to your website.
>
> **Blog**: a type of informal or discussion-based website in which entries or "posts" are presented to visitors in reverse chronological order. Many blogs are interactive, allowing visitors to leave comments on posts.
>
> **RSS (Rich Site Summary)**: a method of publishing frequently updated information online in a "feed" or "channel" that is specially formatted to be easily accessible. Users can subscribe to an RSS feed if they wish to be automatically updated on new material posted to a blog or website.

ACTION PLAN

Date: _____

What do you understand about websites, blogs, and landing or sales pages?

List some possible platforms you're going to use for your business with their processes.

Create a rough sitemap and plan what things should be included in each page.

Verify and decide if you will do this all on your own or if you're going to need help with a website developing company.

Chapter 11
Social Media

Nowadays, you cannot go anywhere without hearing about Facebook, Twitter, Tumblr, and other large social media networks. Every business seems to have a Facebook page that they want you to follow and like! These social media pages serve as outlets for advertising, talking about products, and sharing personal experiences. Having a business social media page will boost your business and keep your customers up to date on developments.

In this chapter, we're going to talk about social media, its importance in today's society, how to use it, and some of the main social media websites out there.

Keyword:

> **Social Media**: websites, networks, and online communities designed to allow people to create, share, or exchange information, ideas, pictures, and videos.

Why is Social Media Important?

In a world filled with technology, people have found a way to use technology to keep tabs on their friends, weather, and favorite sports teams. Why not use social media to attract attention to your business as well? Many businesses have done this successfully. Think about the last time you walked into a chain supermarket and you saw signs on the cart reading, "Find us on [social media site]." What would you find by "finding" your supermarket on a social media website? Advertisements, of course!

Businesses are quickly picking up on the idea of advertising through social media. If you "like" a business on many social media sites, its ads will start appearing whenever you access that social media site. If what businesses advertise looks good to you, then you might be tempted to go onto their main sites and explore further. It is businesses' intention that every ad will end in sales. The most important part of advertising is putting yourself out there, and social media does just that.

Another factor of social media that affects everyone today is this: almost everyone is on it. From grandchildren to grandparents, most people have a profile on at least one social media website. There are sites catering to different types of people. If you're a business professional, there's a social media site for that. If you're into watching and sharing videos, there's a social media site for that. Whatever your interest might be, there is a social media site catering to you. That is one aspect of social media that makes it a great way to get your business's name out there!

Why You Need Social Media in Business

Share! In our generation, this word has taken a deeper meaning than ever. Just go to any website and see different share buttons that you can't miss. These buttons often encourage us to share an article, photo, or a link to various social media.

Done correctly, social media can empower any business to connect with its customers and improve brand visibility. Here are the following reasons why business can benefit through this channel:

1. Build a strong relationship with customers.
2. Drive traffic to your website.
3. Customers are more receptive.
4. Boosts your site's SEO.
5. Faster response.

Your Business Needs Social Media

Your brand needs all the help it can get. If you're not represented across many social media channels, it's difficult to achieve brand visibility. Today, you have to interact with your followers, thought leaders, tastemakers, and journalists who write on your niche, among others.

How to Use Social Media

Social media is a user-friendly format for those who want to stay in touch with what is going on in the world. Setting up a profile on most major social media sites is free and easy, and as soon as your page goes live (i.e., becomes visible to other people), you can start gathering friends and followers.

The first thing you want to do when finding a social media site is to look at who uses it. You want the site you choose to reflect you and your interests. For example, you wouldn't go on a social media website designed for serious-minded networking professionals if you want to use social media to post funny cat videos. The people on such a site are not there for entertainment but to meet other individuals who share similar career interests.

Once you've found an appropriate social media site, you can set up a profile for yourself or your business. Make sure you provide the information that you would like people to know. If you're creating a business social media page, include the positives of your business, such as good reviews, special discounts, and exclusive sales. Make people want to come to your social media page by providing them with a good reason to.

After you're set up, you can invite people to follow or like your page. You might start out with people you know or with whom you've worked in the past. Build your following by networking with those whom you know and who know you, and you will be able to branch out and create new followers as your business grows. Building a following takes time, but those who are willing to like and follow you will be a great testimony to what you stand for.

Keywords:

Follow: a function on many social media sites that allows users to subscribe to another user, thereby allowing them to more be more easily updated on the "followed" user's new posts or other uploads.

Like: a function on many social media sites that allows users to approve a post, picture, web page, etc. This may be presented as a "like" button or in a similar form, such as a thumbs-up button (in which case, there is sometimes also a thumbs-down option). In some cases, "liking" something may alter your search or advertising results within a social media site.

Post: an entry to a blog, Internet forum, or social media site. Such entries are "posted" or "published."

Social Media Websites

Once you have decided to put your business on social media, you must choose which sites you want to use. There are several options, and while it's okay to be on multiple sites, you have to remember to keep them up to date and check them frequently. Remember that when creating them. If you don't have time for all that social media, then you might want to limit your profiles to a few key sites. Let's take a look at some top social media websites.

Facebook

If you haven't heard of Facebook, you may have been living under a rock for many years now. Facebook is the social media giant that has grown so much that it already has billions of users worldwide. It is so well known and popular that it is safe to say that Facebook is the king of social media sites today.

Ideal for Businesses, Not Just Individuals

Facebook is the ideal place for small and medium-sized businesses. Creating your own business page is quick and easy. Once you have your own Facebook business page, you can start growing your followers. People who "like" your page will start receiving your posts on their wall, and they will view your updates or news about your products and services. Facebook users can also "share" your posts or photos, and more and more people will be able to see your posts. This shows the power of Facebook when you want to gain a wider audience or you want some exposure for your new products.

Most business experts believe that continuous interaction and maintaining a good relationship with the customers are very effective in promoting your business. Since Facebook allows you to reply on people's comments regarding your posts, your interaction shows that your business is not just about profits but you also prioritize your customers.

Advantages of Promoting Your Business on Facebook

- Increase your exposure to millions of Facebook users locally and abroad.

- Raise brand awareness.

- Increase traffic to your website.

- Deliver targeted advertising.

- Communicate with customers through videos and photos.

- Facebook is free.

- Respond to people's queries and questions or use it as a customer support.

LinkedIn

LinkedIn is perhaps the most business-oriented social networking site today used by many professionals, companies, and business owners. LinkedIn boasts of having executives from Fortune 500 companies as its members, and millions of companies across the globe have LinkedIn company pages.

LinkedIn can be used to connect with other industry professionals or generate prospects and leads. It can also help you expand your business network or find new talents that can help you in your business.

How to Use LinkedIn for Your Business?

If you already have your own LinkedIn profile, there is already a huge potential to get the attention of potential clients or customers. LinkedIn helps your business get its much-needed exposure because it has a search feature that allows people to find you.

If you want a more proactive approach, you can take advantage of LinkedIn's features.

- You can post important updates that would benefit your customers.

- You can send invitations or messages to people in your network.

- You can join and participate in group discussions related to your business. This gives your business more credibility by showing others that you are knowledgeable in this industry.

Twitter

Twitter is another social media giant that has millions of active users all over the world. It is actually a short-message communication site that falls under the microblogging category, and it allows users to send messages of up to 140 characters to other Twitter members. You can follow other people, and they can also follow you. This will allow you to read their tweets and reply or share their tweets to your followers.

How Is Twitter Used for Business?

You have to create your business profile with the appropriate theme and profile picture. You can choose your business name and have a profile header that shows your line of business. It helps to be proactive in Twitter so that you can gain more attention from your followers. Follow your customers, business partners, suppliers, peers, competitors, professional organizations, and other businesses owned by friends or colleagues.

Twitter is a good medium to drive traffic to your website. You can do this by writing a short, compelling message with your link included. There is a URL shortener in Twitter to save you some space.

Sharing photographs and videos can also be done in Twitter. With the ability to post great-looking photos and videos, you can get the attention of potential customers. This also makes your business look interesting for most people.

Other Social Media Sites that are Useful for Businesses

Aside from Facebook, LinkedIn, and Twitter, which are the three big ones, there are many other social networking sites that can be very useful for your business. If you are more into visuals and you want to promote your products via photographs and videos, you can join YouTube, Instagram, and Pinterest.

YouTube

YouTube is a social media site where users share videos. These videos vary greatly in topic, length, and purpose. Some are informational while others are entertaining. This is a great website to use to give informative explanations of your business and products. You can even have a video blog (or vlog). You do not need an account to watch videos, but you will need one to upload or comment on videos. YouTube is now linked with Google, and you can use a Google+ account as your YouTube account.

Instagram

Instagram is a social media site that allows users to communicate using personal photos and images. Once you are registered on the site, you can upload and view your own photos and easily follow photos posted by other users. The setup is similar to that of other social media sites.

If you market your business in this form, you will want to make sure that your photos are high quality and will sell your product. They must also be appropriate to your audience.

Pinterest

With Pinterest, users can create virtual boards where they "pin" items that they find interesting. These can be anything from recipes to businesses. Users can view one another's boards.

Marketing on this website can help you if you can get people to pin your website on their boards. Word of mouth is a great way to boost sales and create a positive reputation.

How to Connect with Your Audience on Social Media

Have you ever had the experience of speaking ona topic in front of a group of people, and you got the feeling that everything you were saying wasn't being absorbed by your audience? Now let's look at it differently. What if you saw your audience reacting to your words? They engaged with you and asked you all sorts of questions about the topic. It would be a great feeling, right? The connection with your audience would be so deep that it would result in a very engaging discussion, which would give you more credibility and recognition.

It's also the same when you are promoting your business online, especially on social networking sites. You need that deeper connection with your audience if you want your business to succeed and gain credibility. So here are some ways you can connect with your social media audience and reap its rewards.

Find Out Who Your Audiences Are

You cannot connect with your audience if you don't have any idea who they are. Is your target market leaning more toward the younger crowd? Or perhaps you are aiming for those who are 30 and above. Their geographic location is also important because it gives you an idea about their lifestyle and status. Getting to know your audience is important so that you will have a good idea about the types of content you can post on your social media page.

Be a Source of Inspiration

Having a social media account for your business doesn't mean that you only post industry-related content. Sometimes, in order to have a deeper connection with your audience, you also have to be the source of inspiration and motivation for your community. Post something that is very positive, and encourage them with motivational words.

Give Freebies, Discounts, and Great Deals

Everybody loves freebies and discounts. You can make your customers more loyal to your brand and build a strong connection when you provide them with great deals and free offers. Share your promos and deals on social media sites such as Facebook, Instagram, and Twitter and see the positive results.

Be a Trusted Source of Information

Social media has tons of information, but there are only a few that can be considered trustworthy. If you want your business to have more credibility with your audience, you can share accurate industry-related information and data. It's also a good idea to share your insights so you can open up a healthy discussion within the group. You can post the latest industry trends or data that could be helpful for your audience.

These are just some of the ways you can create a strong connection with your audience. There can be other ways as long as you are contributing something positive for your business and your audience. You can offer advice or provide tips and suggestions for your audiences. Always focus on sharing engaging content that can influence people and help your business grow.

Social Media Etiquette and How to Avoid Being Labeled as SPAM

Everyone loves social media nowadays. Why wouldn't we? If you want to learn about someone else's life, you can do it on your monitor or your phone's screen. Having difficulty contacting someone across the globe? Try social media websites and you'll be delighted with the many ways for you to communicate. This is what the digital era has brought us. We definitely adore social media, but there are also other reasons why we come to hate it! Just slightly.

Social Media Etiquette

Many people using social media lack the etiquette required for it to be a safe and enjoyable environment. Ever wake up and check your social media feeds only to be bombarded with nonsense posts, image tags, and group chats? With just a few clicks, and there you have it, you're spamming someone's feeds. If only people could have an invisible filter in their gadgets to screen their posts and messages, social media websites would be a better world. However, in reality, we only have this checklist for you to guide you when promoting your business, before clicking that "post" or "send" button.

Here are some questions you should ask yourself before posting:

1. Is this appropriate on a social media website, or is this best communicated in another way?

2. Will everyone understand this post, or is it too vague, which will cause confused reactions?

3. Have I spell checked the post?

4. Am I using the post as an emotional outlet? Is there a different outlet better for that?

5. Will this post offend anyone? If so, does it matter?

6. Am I posting too much today? (Posting more than three times daily can be excessive.)

7. Am I targeting a specific demographic with this message?

8. Is this post relevant, or is it just relevant to me?

9. Am I okay with absolutely anyone seeing this post?

10. Am I using too much "text-speak" and so many abbreviations that it reads unprofessionally?

11. Do I really want to share this, or am I just venting?

12. Is the post well thought out?

Run through these 12 questions every time you have something to post or you want to promote your business through social media. You'll be happy you have checked before sharing with the world.

Don't Spam

Another issue in this digital era is spamming. Yes, you want to promote your business online, but you have to be vigilant of how you're doing it. There are hundreds of reasons why your promotion, be it email or on social media, might be marked as spam. In fact, it used to favor email marketing as it was the primary tool of communication before. When email filters became sophisticated, it moved to a new target, which is social media networks.

Moving Forward with Social Media

There are many more social media websites out there. In this chapter, I only included a few of the most popular ones to give you an idea about what they are and how they can be used to build exposure to your business. Take some time and look at the Internet yourself to find other social networks that will fit the niche of your business.

Social media is an ever-changing way to connect with people from all over the world. It is one area of pop culture that is not going to die away anytime soon. If you want to sell your business and your product, having profiles on one or more of these websites is a must. Take some time and figure out where your business would gain the most exposure. Just keep in mind that you must maintain every profile you set up.

ACTION PLAN

Date: _____

In your own words, define what social media is and how it can particularly help with your business.

Choose some social media websites that you want to start with and list them in a tabular form with pros and cons for each for easy comparison. Pick out the best three social media sites that can be beneficial for your business.

What affiliate marketing network are you going to use? Are you going to use one or a combination of two or more? Why?

List ways for you to gain a wider audience and more followers as well as ways to prevent being labeled as a spammer on social media sites.

Chapter 12
Putting It All Together

At the beginning of this book, I said that even the smallest of things begins with a vision. Before you go any further, stop and take a moment to visualize what you'd like to do in the future. Visualize your passion, that hobby or skill that you love doing more than anything else. Now visualize yourself turning that passion into a business.

Starting a new business can seem daunting, but I promise you that it is doable. Just take it one step at a time, without ever losing sight of your vision. Keeping your dream in mind will help give you momentum and focus, two elements that will push you through difficult times.

Starting your own home-based business may seem like a scary idea in the beginning. However, startup businesses nowadays can be considered lucky, as they are surrounded with the necessary tools, materials, and skills that they need in order to promote what they offer to their target markets. If you know where to look and how to use your resources, starting a successful business may not be as difficult as you may think.

Some of the most successful businesses today started from the proprietor's own home. A perfect example is Baby Einstein, which is a book series as well as videos that aim to teach children about language, music, poetry, art, and more. Julie Aigner-Clark started the business in her basement, and it eventually grew into a profitable business over the years. With the right mindset, driven attitude, innovative product, and proper promotional tools, you can create a successful home-based business on your own.

Before starting your own venture, you must first ask yourself the following questions:

- Am I good at what I do?

- Is my product or service a necessity?

- Do I have a target market?

- Will I make money out of the product or service I plan to offer?

- Do I have time to manage the business?

- What are my future plans for the business?

Asking these important questions can help assess whether or not you are fit to be a home-based business owner. If you do not have faith in your own product or service, you will have a hard time selling it to your target market. If you cannot devote enough time and effort to your startup business venture, it will be difficult for you to grow it.

To help you along, here is a brief summary of what you must do to achieve your dream of turning your passion into your business:

Starting a Home-based Business

It is normal to be confused about how or where you are going to put up your own business. One helpful step in creating a business is to evaluate your capabilities. Evaluate yourself and identify what makes you think you can succeed in running a venture. Ask yourself if you have what it takes to lead the business to where you want it to be in the future. Creating a plan can also help you have a direction on how you are going to approach your goals.

Have the Right Attitude

Thinking about owning a business is different from running an actual business. Once the actual business is already set up, it is time for you to step up and put your game face on. In order to succeed, you must have the right attitude when it comes to running a business full time. Dedication and passion are important attitudes in order to run a full-time home-based business. Without these traits, you may lose your spark and drive to continue on.

Play According to Your Strengths

When starting a home-based business, it is important to play according to your strengths. Your talents are your biggest asset, which is why you have to utilize them. Are you good with words? Do you enjoy writing? You can use your writing skills to start a blog and attract various readers. You can eventually use your blog to generate income through sponsorships and advertisements.

If you love writing, why not write an e-book? If you are an expert in a particular area, you can create an e-book that can help your readers. This is what Lucinda Cross did, the author of "Corporate Mom Dropouts." Being an experienced work-from-home mother, she created a book that aims to empower women who are thinking about leaving their corporate jobs in order to stay at home and care for their families. Your e-book can be about anything, as long as you know what you are talking about.

If you are always online and have a talent for convincing other people, you can try your luck at affiliate marketing. You can optimize your earnings through the use of the Pay Per Click system, where you get paid for every visitor who clicks on the links that you provide. This is ideal for those who have an expanded network and a wide following.

Using What You Have

Resourcefulness is one of the characteristics that set entrepreneurs apart from others. It is crucial to make the most out of what you currently have and work your way up with it. Just like with any other startup venture, having limited resources is one of the biggest challenges. Limited manpower, limited materials, and of course, limited capital. Therefore, as a starting entrepreneur, you have to learn how to maximize everything you have.

Think of innovative ways to create more without it costing more. Always drop your expenses to a minimum and avoid any kind of unnecessary costs. Minimize costs without compromising the quality of the product or service that you are offering. It may seem like an impossible task, but you will eventually get to where you want your business to be.

The Power of the Internet

The Internet is a very powerful tool when it comes to promotion and advertisement. Almost everyone has access to an Internet connection, which is why it is helpful to use it to expose your business. Let your brand be noticed through the Internet. Create an official website where you can easily post your products and services anytime. Maintain a blog where your consumers can read more about your company as well as your future plans for your business. Remember to keep all information relevant in order to keep your readers and potential buyers interested.

Social Media is Your Friend

Social media has become a great part of consumers' daily lives. Many small businesses have been able to gather enough customers and regular buyers with the help of social media sites and apps such as Instagram, Facebook, Twitter, Pinterest, and more. Through these sites, startup businesses are able to show their products and services to a diverse mix of consumers.

Creating enticing content is very important when it comes to social media promotion. Posting creative and attractive pictures on Instagram, Pinterest, and Facebook can really help pique the curiosity of your audience. Social media sites are free, which is why all businesses, whether they are already established or just starting, should fully utilize them. You get the chance to speak with a wide audience without paying for anything.

132

Embrace Failure

Failure is inevitable, especially when running a business. You cannot create a new business successfully without experiencing any kind of letdown during the process. Prepare to experience a bad customer feedback or even a loss in your revenues. However, do not let them hinder you from succeeding. Learn from your mistakes and accept them. Your failures can help your business improve and become better.

Keep On Learning

Once you are successful in launching your startup business and gathering a number of loyal customers, make sure you do not stop there. Owning a business is a continuous learning process, where the business owner does not stop learning. Remember that there is always room for improvement. Always be on your guard and study your competitors. Look for areas where you can improve your business and your products or services. Find areas that you can help improve. Continuously create innovative products that can help make your customers' daily lives easier. It is essential to maintain the drive and how dedicated you are when you were just starting your business, as it will serve as your fuel to create more and become more successful.

ACTION PLAN

Date: _____

Write down the ways you will get started promoting your business online. Break the plan down into achievable parts.

Create plans on how you will start with e-book writing, affiliate marketing, setting up your own website, and promoting in social media.

List some possible learning curves as well as failures you may encounter in the process and include what you can do with it under your control.

Finalize your plans of promoting your business online.

Glossary

Affiliate Marketing: a process by which a business earns commissions by promoting the products of other businesses.

Backlink: a link from another website connecting a visitor to your website.

Blog: a type of informal or discussion-based website in which entries or "posts" are presented to visitors in reverse chronological order. Many blogs are interactive, allowing visitors to leave comments on posts.

Business Type: the structure or setup by which a business operates, both practically and legally. There are four common options: corporation, limited liability company (LLC), sole proprietorship, and partnership.

Business Venture: an activity pursued for the sake of money. A business venture provides you with a significant portion of your income. Business ventures are pursued during your work time. A business venture may grow out of a hobby.

Change: the active state of turning your new perspective into your new reality. This usually involves stepping out of your comfort zone.

Comfort Zone: also called a "box" or "shell," your comfort zone encompasses the situations and interactions that create within you a safe, easy, in-control feeling. When in your comfort zone, you will have a limited number of thoughts, behaviors, and learning opportunities available, and change will be difficult. One of the first steps to improving your life is to learn how to step out of your comfort zone.

Corporation: a business type that uses shares in which liability is separate from employees and shareholders. Corporations are taxed separately from their owners. C corporations have unlimited shares and are worldwide. S corporations have limited shares that must stay in the hands of United States citizens.

Domain Name: a way of identifying a group of associated web pages. For example, all web pages within a specific website will have the same domain name. In many cases, websites have domain names easily associated with their names. The domain name of the website Amazon is amazon.com.

Dreams: your huge, overarching, or ultimate goals. Dreams do not have to be finite; they can be an ongoing process.

E-book: an electronic book that may be read on a computer, smartphone, e-reader, or other electronic device.

Editing: a service in which the customer pays a professional editor to improve a book. There are different types of editor, so make sure you do some research before hiring one.

Follow: a function on many social media sites that allows users to subscribe to other users, thereby allowing subscribers to be more easily updated on the "followed" user's new posts or other uploads.

Ghostwriting: a service in which the customer pays a professional writer to write a specific book. Traditionally, ghostwriters are not credited for their work.

Goals: stepping stones or achievements that contribute to fulfilling your purpose. Setting both small, reasonable goals and large, overarching goals (or "dreams") can help motivate you.

Hobby: a pursuit of passion for its own sake. A hobby will not provide you with a significant source of income. Hobbies are done in your free time.

Home-based Business: any business in which the primary administrative work (and often the rest of the work as well) is done from the owner's home.

Information-based Product: a type of product used for the purpose of distributing information. Information-based products may be intangible (e.g., commercials), tangible (e.g., books), or services (e.g., history lessons).

Intangible Product: a type of product produced by a business. Intangible products do not require action from the business from which they are purchased, and they do not have physical presence. Examples of intangible products are insurance policies and digital music.

Keyword Research: the practice used to optimize results in a search engine. By choosing attractive and informative keywords to describe your product, you can make that product easier for potential customers to find.

Landing Page: a type of web page. This is the home page of any website. It is designed to be the first page viewers come across when accessing a website and functions much like a book cover by giving viewers a basic overview of what to expect in the rest of the website. Landing pages traditionally also give users easy access to other web pages within a website. Some websites have a pre-landing page called a "splash page."

Liability: legal responsibility.

Like: a function on many social media sites that allows users to approve a post, picture, web page, etc. This may be presented as a "like" button or in a similar form such as a thumbs-up button (in which case, there is sometimes also a thumbs-down option). In some cases, "liking" something may alter your search or advertising results.

Limited Liability Company (LLC): a business type with limited liability in which personal and business assets are separate. LLCs are taxed like individuals or sole proprietorships, not corporations.

Motivation: a combination of momentum and focus. Motivation is what keeps you going—what keeps you fulfilling your purpose.

Partnership: a business type in which multiple individuals own, operate, and have full liability for the business.

Passion: your fuel. The thing you have passion for is the thing you are really good at and really love, and it drives you forward. Passion creates a motivation feedback loop.

Perspective: how you view the world and yourself. By changing your perspective, you can change your personal reality.

Post: an entry to a blog, Internet forum, or social media site. Such entries are "posted" or "published."

Purpose: your purpose is to pursue your passion. This pursuit will include many small goals and one or more dreams.

Reality: the state of affairs and being that is real and actual. Reality is defined both by cultural consensus and by personal perspective. How you perceive your situation and self affects your actual situation and self. In order to change your reality, you need to first change your perspective.

RSS (Rich Site Summary): a method of publishing frequently updated information online in a "feed" or "channel" that is specially formatted to be easily accessible. Users can subscribe to an RSS feed if they wish to be automatically updated on new material posted to a blog or website.

Sales Page: a type of web page that actively sells a product. It typically includes product name, product description, product image, product price, and a "buy now" or "add to cart" button that allows visitors to purchase the advertised product.

Self-confidence: believing in yourself. The first step to self-confidence is to stop thinking negative and/or defeatist thoughts about yourself.

Service: a type of product produced by a business. Services are actions taken by a business on behalf of a paying client. Examples of services are dog walking and academic tutoring. In some cases, services may produce tangible products (such as a photographer who then sells physical copies of the photos taken) or intangible products (such as a photographer who then sells digital copies of the photos taken).

Social Media: websites, networks, and online communities designed to allow people to create, share, or exchange information, ideas, pictures, and videos.

Sole Proprietorship: a business type in which a single owner owns, operates, and has full liability for the business.

Splash Page: a specific type of pre-landing page that contains only a graphic, such as a product image or business logo, on which users must click to access the landing page. In some cases, splash pages are used to allow visitors to pick their preferred language.

Tangible Product: a type of product produced by a business. Tangible products do not require action from the business from which they are purchased, and they have a physical presence. Examples of tangible products are chairs and automobiles.

Visualization: a technique in which you imagine your future self achieving your goals in order to achieve a specific outcome. This mental exercise helps give you the initial energy needed to follow your passion. Visualization alone is not enough for success; it must be followed by action.

Web Page: a web document suitable for the Internet. In simpler terms, it is any individual screen viewable on a website.

Website: a set of associated web pages functioning under the same domain name. Websites are extremely useful tools for marketing to an Internet-savvy customer base.

www.ingramcontent.com/pod-product-compliance
Lightning Source LLC
Chambersburg PA
CBHW020156200326
41521CB00006B/399